FRANKIE HOWERD
THE ILLUSTRATED BIOGRAPHY

FRANKIE HOWERD
THE ILLUSTRATED BIOGRAPHY

Mick Middles

HEADLINE

First published in Great Britain in 2000 by
Headline Book Publishing

1 3 5 7 9 10 8 6 4 2

Copyright © Essential Books 2000

A catalogue record for this title is available from the British Library

ISBN 0 7472 3943 6

Printed in Italy by Canale & C. S.p.A.

Headline Book Publishing
A division of Hodder Headline
338 Euston Road
London NW1 3BH

CONTENTS

INTRODUCTION: THE AGE OF INNOCENCE
'WELCOME TO THE SEXY 70S'

I recall a certain thirteen-year-old *frisson* as that headline crashed into my head, and the 1970s began. Even then I knew it: all manner of wonderment lay ahead. The 1960s had belonged to our older brothers and sisters. We had read, with bewilderment, tales of free love and poetry and weird psychedelic rock festivals full of nude, hairy people slapping about in mud lakes, smoking things, saying 'maan' a good deal and talking with absurd mid-Atlantic affectation.

They had, they said repeatedly, paved the way. They had smashed down the barriers and sexual liberation had been allowed to swamp everyone. I liked the sound of that. How better to inflame the sexual imagination of the bewildered and dim thirteen-year-old than to promise him a decade of rampant sexual experimentation? How lucky we were. What would it have been like, one has often wondered, to be that age as the 1990s opened in a deadening mess of political correctness? What promise lay ahead for those poor latter-day unfortunates? Ten years of boy bands, of girl bands, of mixed boy and girl bands. A tedious barrage of juvenile, cartoon-like pop.

As to the thirteen-year-old's sexual stimulation in the post-PC 1990s? Well, it was there. The flash of an All Saints tummy exiting from some London

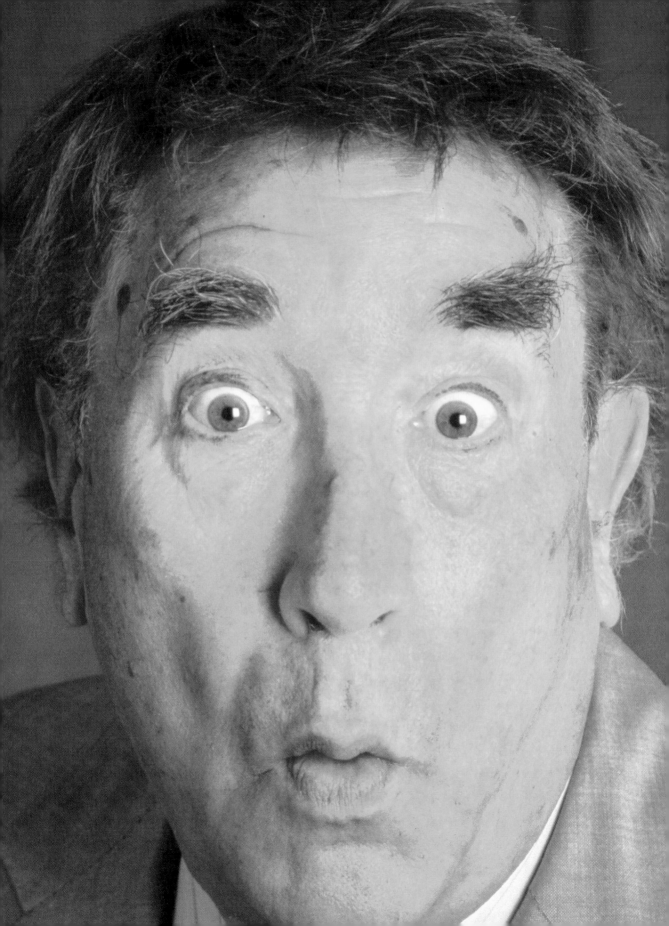

nightclub. Some sun-scorched actress wandering in bikini-clad state across the beach at Summer Bay. Oh, and lots of things, from the diluted gobstopper porn of *Loaded* to, eventually, Claire from Steps. From Anthea Turner to Britney Spears. All a bit boring, really. And within the bounds of comedy things were and are even worse. Ever since Jo Brand constructed monologues about menstruation . . . well . . . the magic had gone. Thirteen-year-olds, one senses, have little to learn about sex; it has all become so pragmatic.

In 1970, things were simpler. Romantic, even. There was still a cloud of mystery, a reason for sexual subversion. It was the *promise* of sex, the infinite possibilities and the myth of harmless sex that could be found all over the place. From the posters of Julie Ege that lined every adolescent male's bedroom walls to the fantastic evolvement of double AA films – films that allowed young bucks over 14 but under 18 to slink into the back rows and sample cinematic sex, even in five-minute sequences in dreadful Western spoofs like *El Condor*. It didn't matter. It was sex. It was brilliant. You saw it and you boasted about it the next day in the playground. Girls, too. Yes, girls too!

And then there was television, which was nothing like the multi-channelled kaleidoscope of today. In 1970, television funnelled down through three channels of, unless you were very lucky, black'n'white mundanity. That said, as a medium, it was astonishingly powerful. It is often noted that, until the mid-1980s, one only had to make one daft appearance on *Top of the Pops* to achieve a weird kind of immortality. Think, say, of Billy J Kramer. Then think of, I don't know, China Crisis. Names forever buried in the nation's psyche. You didn't have to do much, just appear for five minutes and you were 'in'. In the 1990s, by stark comparison, it was possible to achieve fifteen top ten hits and still nobody had a bloody clue as to who you were. Perhaps that was no bad thing. Television, in gaining a broad base, had lost its sheer power of penetration. (Frankie Howerd would have made much of that phrase.) But in 1970, it held the nation in the palm of its hand. Everybody watched everything – at least, that's how it seemed. There was no such thing as a micro-celeb then, no tenth-rate chef or nipple-flashing garden designer desperately clinging to a modicum of fame. No, if you were in the public eye then, you were in the eye of every living thing on the planet. You were regarded as a special being. Yes, I know our starry-eyed state was the product of simple naïveté, but it's just that it was much more fun.

Which is how we come to Frankie Howerd. The world has changed, irreversibly, since 1970. If, today, Frankie Howerd appeared at 9.30pm on a Thursday night and delivered his usual barrage of appalling, brazen, hugely entertaining innuendo, it might cause a little ripple in the *Guardian*'s television column and might even gain some tabloid exposure, but it wouldn't mean anything, simply because it would have to compete with a thousand other forms of communication. But, in 1970, there was simply no competition.

All year, 1970 was dark. I don't think we had a summer. I'm sure Met Office records would suggest otherwise, but it always seemed like winter, or it did in Stockport, where I lived. In blackness. Beneath yellow street lights. Teenagers would huddle on street corners and dream of sex, then return home, at nine, freezing, still dreaming, grasping a milky Horlicks to settle down with parents as Frankie Howerd's *Up Pompeii* hit the television screen.

Looking back, I can't believe all this happened. Sitting on that vinyl pouffe! Soaking in a tidal wave of the risqué and the brazenly naff, with parents chuckling away as if it was all so inoffensive. And it was. It had to be, otherwise they wouldn't allow it on the TV, would they? Nobody believed in the possibility of subversion, not in 1970. In 1970, we trusted people. We trusted our television bosses and we trusted our comedians. We laughed at them, too. Even when they were delivering lines like, 'Hey there – orgy girl.'

Frankie Howerd was a fantastic paradox, especially in *Up Pompeii*. Here he was, as Lurcio, heavy in servitude and yet in control. Accepting his humble stature and yet possessing a curious wry chippiness. As camp as a boy scout jamboree and yet emitting a craggy, dusty, schoolteacherish aura. Sexually repressed and surrounded by scantily-clad goddesses dispensing sexual favours this way and that. Old and boyish. Full of cheek. Full of sarcasm. Full of gorgeous and dreadful punning, lost in an awkward maze of naked innuendo.

For thirty-five minutes each Thursday, English people slumped into their sofas or crouched on their pouffes and allowed their celebrated reserve to evaporate. It was a simple guffaw-fest. Nothing remotely taxing would ever happen. This was carrying on from *Carry On*. Quite literally, as it happened, because the first thirteen episodes were written by stalwart *Carry On* scribe, Talbot Rothwell. The series – lumpenly half-inched from Richard Lester's 1966 movie *A Funny Thing Happened on the Way to the Forum*, starring Zero Mostel, via its earlier theatre incarnation – had been specifically wrapped around the central talents of Howerd. As Lurcio, he would relate each episode's plot, such as it was, directly to the studio audience/camera/thirteen-year-old sitting on a pouffe at home. It was all so simplistic and chummy, like sharing a dirty joke with a dubious uncle who always smelled of whisky and fags. You felt as if you were in on something.

Your mother made you another coffee and smiled as Lurcio chastized the errant daughter, Erotica (played by Georgina Moon). Ludicrous: 'Dear child, so delightfully chaste.' Lurcio: 'Yes . . . and so easily caught!'

The forces of feminism of the day attacked the show of course and, like other, similarly themed shows, *Up Pompeii* would eventually be driven from the airwaves. But we knew it would be back. We knew the stupidity lay in not seeing the joke. Or, indeed, in failing to see, deep in the psyche of Howerd, an extraordinary respect for women. How ridiculous it now seems.

None of this was quite an issue in the ever-so-much simpler times of 1970, though. Elsewhere on television, one might stumble across Richard Beckinsale and Paula Wilcox, casting adoring looks at each other over shared butties in Manchester's Albert Square in *The Lovers*. ('Geoffrey Bobbles Bon Bon' sighed Paula's Beryl and we, the thirteen-year-olds, simply died.) We also had *The Kenny Everett Explosion*, *The Comedians* (in 1971, a relentless barrage of northern comedians jovially chastizing 'the Missus') and Diana Dors as the matriarchal Queenie in *Queenie's Castle* (a Yorkshire mum who controlled her family with a fist of iron). Political correctness never entered into anything. We just soaked it in and laughed, in all innocence.

I looked at the girls, too, loads of them. Bosomy and bossy. Flitting around the central force of Lurcio's disdain. In this book, we will not heap lumps of social meaning onto all that – it was, after all, adult panto. I was giggling helplessly by the time the entire *Pompeii* set seemed to shudder like a *Star Trek* craft under attack. And that was another thing about *Up Pompeii*. It was always so obviously, so deliberately, taking place in a television studio. More than that, it was a swiftly painted set that had been made by the cast of *Blue Peter*, probably, and hastily shoved together to crudely resemble stone slabs, marble, statuary and spa steps. Well, anything vaguely Roman would do. There are pizzerias in Pontefract that evoke a more Roman atmosphere than that set. It was farce, mate, farce through and through and, in this slick new century, with all manner of computer trickery capable of summoning whole other worlds onto our televisions – think *Walking with Dinosaurs* which was technically brilliant, meticulously researched and unbearably tedious – one cannot help but miss it. Oh, for the English amateurism which typified *Carry On*. For mad, daft innuendo. For genuinely talented people, creating a little warm mirth with sex as a comedic device, nothing more, nothing less. Of course, this is all a personal nostalgic dream. The thing is though, I felt that I understood Frankie. It wasn't difficult. It was the sardonic acceptance of just how utterly absurd the world was, in Pompeii as in Peckham. One might as well laugh and go with the flow. Have a laugh, ogle a bit, then slink off to bed.

Of course, the rest of the 70s weren't quite as sexy as had been forecast. Well, they might have been, elsewhere, but it didn't quite gel in Stockport. Frankie Howerd seemed to set it all up for me but girls with names like Julie and Yvonne never lived up to the promise of Erotica. Indeed, by contrast, they were manipulative, financially motivated and decidedly untrustworthy. Lurcio didn't prepare me for any of that. He didn't prepare me for real life. I suppose that was a bit of a disappointment. I recall seeing an older, rather dour Mr Howerd on a latter-day television chat show, *Aspel* I think, and he concluded that '. . . *Pompeii* was a load of bollocks and bristols'.

Yes, it was precisely that. Funny how I miss it, though.

CHAPTER 1
KENTISH CAPERS

It was the beautiful and unsuspecting city of York that welcomed Francis Alick Howard (the 'a' in his surname would be replaced by an 'e' for professional reasons many years later) to the world, in the midst of the First World War which still showed no end in sight, in 1917. He wasn't born to the swank and glory of the Georgian houses that stretched from the city perimeters out into the flat surrounding Yorkshire countryside, but rather to the other side of town. The Howards lived among the small cluster of two-up, two-downs which spilled down to the River Ouse. Although Frankie would later refer to it as 'poor', and the Howards certainly had to scrimp in the grim post-war manner so much of Britain had to endure, it was several steps beyond the poverty that gripped the larger, darker cities of Britain. Both his parents worked. His father was a sergeant in the Royal Artillery while his mother, like many York mothers then as now, worked in the manufacture of chocolate. A noble occupation.

As the family moved to south London within three years of his birth, Francis's memories of York amounted to little more than a tumble down the house stairs, hilariously recounted in his 1977 memoir, *On the Way I Lost It*.

The new family home was in Eltham, Kent – the birthplace of Bob Hope. Today the London encroachment has long since swallowed this hamlet, reducing it to little more than another square on the intricate pattern of the *A to Z*. But in 1920, Eltham retained a semi-rural status. Even compared to York, it provided a pleasant, ubiquitous backdrop where young Francis grew up in the comfort of lower-middle-class anonymity. Despite soon being blessed by a sister, Bettina, and a brother, Sidney, Francis remained a solitary, curiously shy child who found it difficult to make friends and mostly preferred to wander alone among Kentish fields, or sit in his room, devouring comics, listening intently to his mother's casual renditions of show songs and radio hits.

He attended, tentatively, Gordon Elementary School and there are no reports of him achieving anything that might set him apart from the ordinary. He was happy enough, sitting with a tight circle of friends, cowed by the omnipresent threat of the cane. He was introduced to the magic of the theatre when his mother took him to the Woolwich Artillery Theatre – where his father was stationed – and he excitedly soaked in the frenetic atmosphere of panto. Nearly fifty years later, speaking on Radio 4, he would exclaim, 'I never lost my sense of wonder about pantomime from that day. It transported me to another world. That's all you can ask of any theatre.'

The visit signalled the initial stirrings of a vocation. Francis Howard, at home, began building cardboard theatre sets. He began writing simplistic plots and staged many living-room floor shows, none of which apparently made much impression on his siblings. This would develop over the years and, with the help of the local kids' posse, he began staging concerts in his back garden and then in the back gardens of school friends. It is, perhaps, tempting to make much of this but, as Howard later admitted, 'It was just something that kids did.' Talent was still buried deep beneath childhood bravado. Although his mother was surprised by his lack of inhibition, when he was 'performing' on that lawn, he was still essentially a child whose shyness lay at the edge of introversion.

Howard proudly attended Shooter's Hill Grammar School. Passing his 11-

WELLINGTON PIER PAVILION
GREAT YARMOUTH

SOUVENIR
PROGRAMME

Frankie Howerd
Laugh Show

Oh, he did like to be beside the seaside; a programme from the early 1960s

plus exam was quite an achievement for a comparatively poor child, and he seemed to settle in quickly, excelling at maths and stumbling over Latin, a subject he correctly regarded as absurd and wholly superfluous. His imagination was stirred by Sunday School where soon he was spinning his own, not entirely biblical, tales into weekly monologues. It was here that something extraordinary seemed to happen: Francis discovered a talent for holding the attention of his fellow students. Something which was not necessarily shared by the older teachers, who often performed in a less colourful manner. Although nobody made much of a fuss of this small triumph, Howard himself regarded it as a major breakthrough in his young life. He realized two things. First that, with a little preparation the previous night, he could prepare a story that would lock into the imagination of his fellow pupils. And second, that the nervousness that would accompany his storytelling, which often forced him to fall into an initially embarrassing stammer, could be used to dramatic effect. It was early days indeed, but the basis of Howard's act, if that is not too demeaning a word, was already starting to form. As he would later state, 'Never knew where it came from, this thing that I do. It just descended upon me. I was stuck with it.'

Young Francis made various and not entirely successful attempts to filter his stammering technique into school plays and even became one of the leading lights in Gordon's depleted Dramatic Society. Later, he would claim to have been damned with affectation during this spell as, in contrast to his schoolfriends who seemed content to drift towards accountancy, he saw his career path spiralling ever upwards, towards that most noble of occupations, acting. His naiveté only served to encourage his quest. He complemented his school play activity with extra lessons at the London County Council Dramatic Society and, approaching sixteen, even caught a glimpse of a place at RADA. It might be noted that this initial career plan, and the way it was crushed when the RADA place failed to materialize, is duplicated in the biographies of a thousand British thespians. In Howard's own book, *On the Way I Lost It*, he recalls, 'Never before or since have I wept as I did on that day.' This is a recognizable state for most mid-teens, when the world fails to unfold in exactly the manner the spotty oik might expect. For Howard, who stopped to cry his eyes out in a field on the way home, the profound disappointment was in fact a blessing. So hurt was he, that the notion of Francis Howard, Shakespearean 'acktooar' – which, in retrospect, doesn't seem so absurd – was brusquely swept aside. He knew right there, in the Kentish countryside, that he had enough talent to break through and make a living from acting. But it would have to be through comedy. Howard would often recall that moment, when he made his choice.

Leaving school in 1933, hell-bent on comedic fame, he started a filing job in London's thriving industrial docklands. It wasn't hard work and, as soon as he had mastered the office routine, he allowed himself to operate on automatic while his mind raged through comedy sketches and techniques. Although he would dismiss it as pretentious, he also learned a great deal from studying the idiosyncratic actions of his fellow workers, especially noting the way they fell into a role within the office hierarchy – and not necessarily a role that would suit their personalities. There was a certain absurdity to be gleaned from this. He continued on course for a professional showbiz life by embarking on the amateur dramatic circuit. It was, again, a time he'd never forget; equally, he'd never deride the amateur performers. In fact, for Howard, it was a hugely enjoyable learning curve. Performing for no money allowed him the freedom to develop without having to accept the usual responsibilities of a professional actor. He filtered his energy into his night-time activities, eventually taking control of his local dramatic society and using it as a base to expand the revues he wrote while flitting from office to office and filing job to filing job.

As you might expect, the 'venues' in which Howard built his act were not on the normal itinerary for testing stage talent; there was an old folks home in Catford, in the mid 1930s, where The Frankie Howard Comedy Revue or Frankie Howard Knockout Concert Party would be performed with the star of the show surrounded by a disparate huddle of supporting cast: eager beavers, but lacking Howard's talent and drive. It must have been quite a sight: the

bewildered octogenarians gaping as Howard told the circulating jokes of the day, moulding them to suit his personality. By some accounts he even adapted the unfunny ones – somehow, through his increasingly hilarious, stuttering delivery, bringing them alive.

Howard's night-time work rate was little short of extraordinary. He was 'driven' to the point of obsession, his ambition forcing him, time after time, to clamber onto the stage – *any* stage. He wouldn't relax at weekends, when he would force his way into the 'talent nights' that featured in the clubs and variety halls of south London. It was here that the real 'Frankie Howerd' was forged during these nights of hard, cold performances, as he cobbled together a succession of jokes with which to attack a largely apathetic crowd, or interspersed his jokes with a series of impressions. Without treading any innovative ground whatsoever, he was by now perfecting the art of impressionism. He particularly enjoyed the way he could catch the audience's attention by unleashing a barrage of Cagney-esque falsetto. Although he would later talk that particular talent down, saying in his autobiography that he 'couldn't do impressions. It was a disaster,' reports suggest he was actually rather good. Certainly the disparate parts to his evolving act were gaining him a reputation for producing the unexpected. There were occasional disasters, embarrassing stage 'deaths', but these would simply add to his experience and help him hone his act. There was, though, a possible danger. His frenetic activity on the amateur circuit could easily have cemented him within those boundaries. He was becoming too well known locally and he desperately needed some kind of break into the wider showbusiness arena.

Aware that he needed to move on but unsure how to, he had to continue performing as he was. It is a cliché but the true spice of Frankie's act lay not in his choice of material, but in the battle that raged within him, between the shy boy and the adult determined to prove his talent. It was a fight he appeared to be winning, for his shyness and stage nerves actually provided him with a definite edge. He'd never defeat those nerves – they would later gain him a reputation for pre-performance surliness – but he would learn to control them.

CHAPTER 2
A TONIC FOR THE TROOPS

By the year 1940, the Second World War had begun in earnest and Francis Howard found himself on a totally new stage. Army life plucked him from his showbiz dream and forced him to help defend Southend by initially stationing him at Shoeburyness Barracks. He and his equally dumbfounded fellow new recruits must have made a fearsome sight, huddling on the sand dunes, ready to pounce should German armed forces find their way across the Channel. The ramshackle nature of British defence at the start of the war – the entire army, let alone the Home Guard – would later work its way into the heart of British post-war comedy. Of course Britain fairly quickly forced itself into a new, battle-ready sophistication; still later on, in films, revues and sitcoms, the entertainment industry was allowed proudly to admit that, for a while back there, things verged on the pathetic.

For his part, Gunner Howard wandered around the Essex coastline, swapping jokes with his friends and wholly unsure what he would do should he ever come face to face with a real live German. Naturally, his greatest role lay in keeping the troops entertained by dominating the barracks concert

parties. Nobody, at Shoeburyness or nearby Wakering, had enough resolve to keep Frankie Howard off the stage. He simply clambered on, and did his bit. Which more often than not would now be little more than a few self-deprecating war references punctuated by a stammering technique that was well and truly becoming his trademark. He didn't know why he was funny. He just was. He could lighten the mood with the flick of his eye. He had invented a camp – in both senses of the word – sarcasm that would curiously twist a concert room full of terrified conscripts into a carefree, rapturous mess.

'No . . . no . . . no look . . . ooooh don't! No, look. Oh, please yourselves.'

Everyone reading this book will, of course, have read the above line in Frankie-speak. And, of course, it's funny. But to read it dry, with no idea of the originator, would evoke nothing but solemn bewilderment. Here's where the essence of genuine comic talent comes in. There's no formula, and no critic in the history of newspaper Arts pages will ever be able to explain it. It's simply talent. It can be honed, sharpened and perfected and it can be ruined and lost, but it cannot be invented or instilled. It belongs to the owner and nobody else, despite what the surrounding contracts might say. Frankie Howard – who now decided to bill himself as Frankie Howerd, was the archetypal example of inexplicable comic genius, a genius unearthed at an apparently incongruous time and place – entertaining the troops, as the Second World War's horrific events unfolded across Europe.

For many of these concert parties, Frankie was ably supported by his sister Betty whose considerable singing talents, not to mention her unselfish support of her extraordinarily gifted brother, might also have provided her with a showbiz career. This she never desired, thus depriving the world of an exceptional sibling double act. Nevertheless, as she surged through 'A Nightingale Sang in Berkeley Square', complete with comedic touches, it was clear there was a talent which flowed through the family.

War or no war, there were a few intriguing excursions. Howerd's talent had started to stretch before him, and invitations – about one a year, probably –

Frankie takes up wrestling . . . with osteopath Robinson in *Man with the Suitcase* drifted gently his way. There was one incredible concert party group, named The Co-Odments, who specialized as a touring party, backfiring around Southend, Chelmsford and Basildon in a battered grey van. (They would make a terrific starting point for a television series, or a Beryl Bainbridge novel.) Howerd treated this new-found and rather odd troupe (they employed a deaf pianist, for example) as a great adventure. Within weeks, he had taken control of the group, often pressurizing them into performing two or three shows a week. It was clear that Howerd was completely devoted to the stage, much to the exasperation of his fellow performers. He became fond, in the most innocent way – because he *was* an innocent, infamous for delivering second-hand innuendo that, although it got him into very deep water, hadn't dented his sexual naïveté – of donning an ATS girl's uniform and, with two burly lads also garbed in low camp, performing the Howerd song, 'Miss Twillow, Miss True and Miss Twit'. It was cheery and cheeky rather than bawdy or rude.

The chummy camaraderie of Essex was inevitably lost as Howerd spent time in an 'Army Experimental Station' on the Gower Peninsula, and then as the Allies prepared to move into occupied Europe, to Plymouth. He was told, and quite cheerily by his own recollection, that he would have to prepare for 'the big show'. This Americanism served only to fill him with dread. The messing about was over. Now for the real thing. He undertook Commando training in Devon and then found himself, as so many did, staggering uncomfortably through France, Belgium, Holland and finally, as the war reached its end, Germany.

Typically, Howerd's post-war army experiences – which he loved to recall on radio shows, from an early *Desert Island Discs* in 1959 through to a Russell Harty Radio 4 Howerd special in 1982 – were peppered with unlikely concert parties in strange, war-torn places. After failing a series of auditions for *Stars in Battledress*, his fortunes seemed to rise when, in Germany, he fell under the command of two influential showbiz icons: Major Richard Stone, latterly a hugely respected theatrical agent, and Captain Ian Carmichael.

There are times, and this was surely one of them, when the future is presented as an obvious path. The two senior army men immediately warmed to Howerd's talent and drive and put him in charge of a concert party that toured the Allied bases of north west Germany. It must have been another bizarre little troupe but at least the mood of victory had eased the dangers of flippancy. As Howerd would later note to Russell Harty, 'I always had a sense during wartime that showbiz had become too fluffy and was an insult to people who were more heavily involved in the war than I was. I was wrong. In many ways the importance of jokes increased in such times, but it was impossible not to feel a little guilty.'

This is wholly understandable. There was also another curious coincidence; during a late spell with the concert party, he worked fleetingly with a young stage manager called Alfred Hill, latterly and more famously known as Benny. However, in true Lurcio style, just as his new role as concert party leader had started to go somewhere, he was demobbed. After six years of army life, he found himself back in Eltham, wearing a pinstriped demob suit and clutching a reference from Richard Stone, which apparently praised him for the quality and enthusiasm of his work with the concert party. Not, perhaps, a typical demob reference, but it would serve Howerd well.

Naturally, he was in a state of some confusion. What to do? How to do it? The London batch of showbiz agents at the time was an enormously dominant breed and breaking into that circle seemed beyond a young hopeful from Eltham, no matter how talented. He did attend interviews but, with no professional work on his CV, found it impossible to sufficiently impress the snootily aloof agents. Even more unsettling was his failure to gain a spot at Butlin's in Filey – launch pad of so many post-war stars – after producing, at the audition, a joke of vague rudeness. Back in Eltham he settled into the greyness of diminishing hope. It was, he would later state, the most depressing period of his life. His brilliant showbiz ambitions were reducing daily as he trudged around London's West End, gazing woefully at the theatres, lost in a seemingly hopeless dream.

His demoralized and rather aimless wanderings served only to highlight the possibility of sinking back into mundane office work. This was a dark and increasingly likely reality for Howerd who sensed that, once he succumbed, he would be condemned to a life where his talent would become little more than a fading hobby. In desperation, he took an illegal step by donning his army uniform and, clutching his reference, turned up at the famed Stage Door Canteen. This was run by the Naafi (Navy, Army and Air Force Institutes) an organization providing canteens, shops and so forth for British Military personnel; at the Stage Door, servicemen and -women offered their services for free, providing acts to support any passing showbiz stars.

Using all the smarm, bluff and bluster that he had learned over the years, he managed to secure a spot for the following week. Although it was little more than a glorified talent spot, it was nevertheless a West End date. At last he could actually invite prospective agents to catch his act. Which he did, only for them not to turn up.

Demoralized, Howerd returned to Eltham intent on submitting to the soulless alternative of office work. To his surprise, however, he was asked back to the Stage Door Canteen the following week and, by chance, not only did he turn in one of his finest performances – his last, he genuinely believed, so he might as well go out with a bang – but he was seen by a representative from an agency fronted by ex-band leader Jack Payne. Two bizarre auditions later and Francis Howard, having firmly adopted the slight alias of Frankie Howerd, entered the world of professional showbiz.

CHAPTER 3
THE KITCHEN SINK COMIC

Sheffield, in 1946, was a hilly swirl of terraces fanning down to a sprawl of heavy industry and a small, slightly daunting, dark city centre. Although it had yet to be blighted by savage chunks of featureless concrete, it was still clawing its way out of soot-blackened poverty. The city centre pubs held tough, unapproachable reputations. In short, it lacked the comforting frivolity of the West End and, although surrounded by the beauty of South Yorkshire and Derbyshire, seemed altogether ugly, unwelcoming and not quite the kind of place that Howerd would have chosen for his professional debut.

Nevertheless, in the summer of 1946, posters were slapped onto Sheffield walls that boasted the arrival of the touring revue, *For the Fun of It*. An evening of jollity for a city dragging itself from the rigours of war. The poster proclaimed the headline act to be the enormously popular singer Donald Peers.

If you took a magnifying glass and studied the poster's bottom edge, you would have discovered the names Frankie Howerd and Max Bygraves (then an optimistic comic and impressionist who, if pressed, would burst into song). Naturally, Howerd and Bygraves fell together with ease. They shared the same downbeat digs, where they would discuss their act over breakfast. By all accounts they stole the show. Bygraves, exuberant and brimming with confidence, was the perfect foil for Howerd, whose nerves were crumbling into a state of career-threatening terror.

On many occasions Bygraves would recall this tour – and never could he understand how an artist as naturally gifted as Howerd could seem so lacking in confidence. Whereas the Bygraves style was to assume a relaxed, almost somnolent posture and thereby set the audience at ease, Howerd would be all edge and stammer – the complete antithesis. They differed in dress as in delivery. Bygraves took the glittery showbiz stance, garbing himself in garish colours; Howerd, somewhat intriguingly, reacted against the showbiz norm and dressed in dour, downbeat suits. The effect was simple. He looked for all the world as if he had just clambered onstage from the stalls.

This innovative stance was fuelled by fear. Howerd found comfort in refusing to adopt the traces of glamour. This 'common man' approach filtered into his act, a full nine minutes, during which he sauntered to the front of the stage, striking a conversational approach like a man entering the tap room at his local – a very nervous, slightly inebriated and ungainly man. The early appearance of the professional Frankie Howerd was nothing if not paradoxical. His look was ordinary and yet slightly mad, like some clumsily brilliant maths professor. He was confrontational but anxious. He was the most natural, unnatural performer on the circuit and though he carried his nerves like a stack of weapons, he never lost control. He couldn't, you see. For even if Frankie Howerd blanked and forgot his entire act, he could make it through an entire nine minutes with little more than a stutter.

'I . . . oh . . . ooohh . . . phew . . . erm . . . ha . . . Oh, don't . . . no, do you . . . no, don't . . oh, suit yourself.'

Max Bygraves would later state that every rule he had painstakingly learned in the honing of his act would be broken by Howerd. This is, of course, another reference to that special something. If you are funny, you can break every rule in the book.

In his autobiography, Howerd referred to himself as a one-man situation comedy – the kitchen sink comic – and, in this description, one senses a striking

modernity. This was a shambling, brown-suited stand-up comic, almost 'alternative' in approach; and this long before Alexei Sayle was even born.

Now that he had an agent – Jack Payne – Howerd's perspective altered. He could relax, concentrate on his act, fall into a warming bonhomie with Bygraves. When you had an actual agent, things happened. Like, for instance, the chance to take his act onto radio, BBC's gloriously named *Variety Bandbox*, in fact. A Sunday Light Programme variety special pinned down by compère Derek Roy, it was big-time. In 1946, radio was a controlling and evocative force, turning disembodied voices into stars. Howerd was thrilled.

He crafted a radio act, mostly pulled from his on-stage show, but with added topical themes. But as he would quickly learn, the problem with radio auditions (and most radio) was the complete and utter lack of atmosphere. That atmosphere, the audience connection, lay out there somewhere, not in an austere BBC studio. It was like performing in a grey shell. Many would take great comfort from such a confined space. Howerd, by contrast, completely lost it and his act fell into a stammering mess of nerves. He was an instant hit.

Two months later, as winter 1946 crept in, Howerd performed his debut radio performance from the Camberwell Palace theatre, which came, mercifully, with its own live audience. The Light Programme adored him from his very first 'Oooh, er, errr, here we are . . .'

Frankie Howerd was up and running. The problem – and this hadn't dawned on him until he walked away from that initial *Variety Bandbox* – was that you couldn't build an act on radio. Like the television phenomenon which was to follow, radio sucked in and dated every joke, every utterance. A whole new act was needed every single week. No jokes could be repeated, refined, twisted and perfected. They were delivered – and suddenly they were out there and gone!

Howerd's radio delivery took a while to perfect. First, he had to adapt to the fast turnover of material, which proved difficult to assess, for there was no way of knowing whether a new joke worked or not. It was simply told, and that was it, no feedback. And second, a dip in listener figures informed him that he was, in fact, wasting half his act. He was still pulling faces, working the live audience, but none of this transmitted through the radio. Although his confidence had mushroomed during his initial three months, and his status as a professional performer had filled him with pride, he began to realize that he still had much to learn.

It was hard work and, even with the help of gags passed to him by Max Bygraves, radio proved an ever-hungry beast, the only compensation being that he could steal bits from the radio to feed into his live act. He had, however, achieved a reasonable level of fame and his growing bag of catchphrases – 'Oh, please yourselves', 'Not on your nelly' – had started to filter into everyday life. That said, life was far from glamorous. He was endlessly shunting through various austere B&Bs on tour before returning, exhausted, to his tiny flatlet in grimy Shepherd's Bush.

It was at this point, as Howerd's extraordinary delivery soaked into the public consciousness, that he began to attract calls and letters from would-be writers. There were many of these and, by his own admission, he never quite got round to seeing them all. Indeed, he even acknowledged that some of the finest comedy writers of the 1950s and 60s might have started their careers with Howerd, had he had the time and patience to see them.

One, however, did manage to slip through the net. In Sheffield, a young, ambitious Eric Sykes burst confidently into Howerd's dressing room, precociously claiming that he would soon be writing for him. His claims proved to be wholly justified. Eric Sykes, while crafting himself a parallel career as a performer, supplied Howerd with a continuous roll of surreal situations, all of which were pinned into place by Howerd's idiosyncratic delivery. The partnership worked superbly and was perhaps more of a bonus than Howerd initially realized.

CHAPTER 4
THE GOOD, THE BAD AND THE DOWNRIGHT RUDE

With the colour supplied by Sykes's relentless invention, the Great British audience was never allowed to become bored by Frankie Howerd's comic persona. The 1950s had yet to begin and Frankie Howerd was already forging ahead. In a reactionary showbiz world as yet unaffected by rock'n'roll, Frankie Howerd was delivering comedy that was surreal and constantly changing.

There were still bad times, though. Howerd would often recall the Glasgow of 1949, a city still deep in the grip of grime and poverty. A wild, unforgiving, razor city, swirling with real violence and just as real desperation. Not a place for a young English comic to attempt to captivate the audience with a courageous rant about his English/Scottish ancestry, especially as the audience missed the point completely and surged to the front, demanding the blood of this, as they saw him, foolhardy Englishman intent on ridiculing the Scots.

The venue was the infamous Glasgow Empire, a legendarily volatile hall which could switch from being heaven to hell in an instant. Halfway through his act Howerd knew he was in trouble and yet, through a tirade of dangerous audience barracking, he stuck doggedly to his task, all too aware that laughter

and applause – aside from slow hand-clapping – were not going to be in any kind of plentiful supply.

He finished and strode briskly from the stage. Eric Sykes would later claim it to be the most courageous act he had ever seen. Certainly, Howerd could leave only after a large gang of young men had finally dispersed. They weren't, he decided, waiting for autographs. The experience weighed heavy on him, but it also taught him the importance of adapting an act to suit different audiences. What might generate uncontrollable hilarity in Southend might just as soon induce total silence in South Shields. It was simply down to experience. Nevertheless, it would be many years before Frankie Howerd would feel at all at ease in Glasgow.

At this time, *Variety Bandbox* was proving to be Howerd's mainstay. On alternate Sundays he would headline, and he was beginning to gain institution status in the slot that would one day be taken up by the pop charts and, before that – depending on your age and how dreadful your taste was – *Sing Something Simple*.

Agents and film companies bombarded the show with their latest crop of stars, all desperate to slide onto the *Variety Bandbox* podium to plug their latest cinematic escapade, alongside Howerd. Every emergent star of the early 1950s would appear, from Dirk Bogarde to Tony Hancock, Billy Butlin to Richard Burton. All happy to read through an Eric Sykes script, all quite prepared to risk being made fun of. It didn't matter. It was *Variety Bandbox* and in an early 1950s kind of way, it was cool.

And it *was* cool. It is difficult now, to imagine a young Frankie Howerd, blessed with dashing looks that were just beginning to crag, as the embodiment of youthful, cutting edge culture. And it's impossible, when listening to the clips, to realize that this was a performer who was thought to be anarchic, especially as his name and image would always seem profoundly reactionary.

It seems like glancing back through a long dark tunnel, to a fading world where sepia-toned figures appear on stage and radio. How ancient it must seem now, to kids growing up with *The Fast Show*. And yet, it's possible to glimpse in *The Fast Show* the distant ghost of *Variety Bandbox*. Fast, pacy delivery, quick-fire gags, game guest stars and topical shadings. The age of modern comedy was well under way.

Howerd's glorious year of 1951 should have been capped by a glorious appearance on the twenty-first anniversary *Royal Variety Performance*, a stalwart radio event soon to attain legendary status as the age of television dawned. For the nervous Howerd, this was one show he both cherished and feared, for its logistical problems were legendary. To pull together top performers from around the world, squeeze their acts into bite-sized chunks and sprinkle them across three hours of non-stop rolling entertainment, must be one of the most difficult stagings in showbiz. Add to this the nervy kudos of performing before royalty, plus the backstage meltdown of dozens of intense, explosive egos and to Howerd you have a disaster waiting to happen.

Every act that has ever performed at the event has had to go through the same rigorous battle with nerves. For every Les Dawson, who stole the show on two memorable occasions, there is a Danny Kaye, who sensationally froze in 1953. Howerd approached the entire affair – which only lasted two days, including rehearsals – with a sense of draining confidence. At the press call he attempted to upstage the other acts by pretending to fall asleep in the plush, comfortable Palladium seats.

He was told he would be closing the first half of the show. It was quite an honour, as it offered secondary headline status, plus it also meant he wouldn't be nervously pacing the dressing room until late in the evening. The only problem was that, due to an extraordinary piece of scheduling, Howerd's closing first-half act would have to follow the bombastic sounds of the Billy Cotton Band, which in those days seemed a more natural 'closer'.

Howerd wandered into the post-Cotton vacuum with diminished confidence, his jittery delivery sounding thin and unconvincing in such a spot. Although the performance was not quite the disaster he described in his autobiography and certainly shouldn't be seen as a dark cloud in his breakthrough years, it was far from the ground-breaking triumph of his

dreams. He managed to raise a few gentle laughs, but the show did seem to dip softly into the interval, hardly the desired effect. Howerd, unable to face the pseudo sympathy of his fellow performers, fled into the Soho night, wandering through the infamous network of streets with little purpose other than to walk through his apparent shame.

Legend has it that he even sauntered into a pub – The Ship in Wardour Street is one of a number of pubs that claimed to be the venue – started chatting with a fan and, cheered, walked straight back to the Palladium for the finale. Although Howerd made no mention of this in his autobiography, other than admitting to the walk, he did refer to the pub incident in a number of radio interviews.

It wasn't the end of the world. It just felt like it for a while.

Jumping for Joy, 1955

CHAPTER 5
THE EXISTENTIALIST

In 1951, after finally leaping from the comfort of *Variety Bandbox*, Howerd once again adopted the writing of Eric Sykes and appeared, alongside a very young Hattie Jacques, on the BBC series *Fine Goings On*, a show wrapped entirely around Howerd's method of delivery and broadcast from the Paris Studios in Lower Regent Street. Later, Howerd would blame the venue for being unsuitable – too small, in the main – for his technique. Undoubtedly, he never felt comfortable in the building but one senses strongly that, for a change, Sykes's writing had failed to support the show's star. Once again, the relative failure was exaggerated by Howerd's reaction, which was to spend time alone in distressed reflection, shunning all helpful advances. This began to earn him a reputation for rapid mood swings, if not surliness. It wasn't affectation, though. His nerves caused his depressions to darken and his highs to surge. Still it was a dangerous situation, because a reputation – however exaggerated – of unsuitability, hardly builds confidence within prospective showbiz bookers.

With Anny Berryer in *Pardon My French* at the Prince of Wales Theatre
Overleaf: (left to right) Frankie Howerd, Toke Townley and
Margaret Rutherford in *The Runaway Bus*, 1953

'Frankie was known for being awkward,' Eric Sykes told Michael Parkinson, 'and that reputation was both understandable and incorrect. Frankie simply needed to have a clear head in order to perform. It was his way of conquering his nerves and, if somebody approached him as he was preparing, he would seem to be a bit sharp. It wasn't in any way malicious or egotistical. He just had to concentrate very hard or he would lose it.'

Some people believed that Howerd 'lost it' during *Fine Goings On*. To some extent, he would have agreed. There is a pivotal scene in his autobiography which sees him, once again, wandering through London streets. This time it was Kensington – a far cry from Soho – and, as he walked, he gazed forlornly at the elegant buildings, the chic shop fronts, the bustling pubs and, not for the first time, he felt pangs of existential dread. People everywhere were simply 'getting on with their lives'.

Yet here he was, a famous person but curiously detached. It was as if he felt like mere entertainment, something that people might pick up for amusement and swiftly put back down again. His job and, for that matter, any entertainer's job, was merely to stretch that period in an enjoyable manner. It was a feeling that surfaced in Frankie Howerd radio and press interviews throughout his long career. Far from feeling like 'the centre of the universe' – which, frankly, is the normal state of celebrity – he felt he was an inconsequential satellite.

'Sometimes I wake up in some hotel and I hear noises – cars, market stalls, factory noises, anything – and I feel lonely. As if I'm not really part of it,' he told the *Sunday Times* in 1974. This statement could be interpreted in various different ways. A lack of ego, perhaps? Or – more likely – as a sure sign of the ongoing battle with nerves which raged within him, a battle that occasionally threatened to swamp his entire personality.

From the thoughts that accompanied his Kensington walk, Howerd crafted the idea of returning to perform for British troops. This time, he'd take Eric Sykes and a small body of BBC recordists to Cyprus, Egypt, Benghazi and Tripoli and write entire concert parties while they were on the move. Slightly bizarre, especially as the resultant 'warts'n'all' broadcasts would surely stretch the Howerd nerves to the limit. But that was the plan – to confront his fears head-on. The method was terrifyingly simple. Cast members would be randomly plucked from nervous RAF personnel, issued with hastily scribbled scripts and shunted in front of an extensive array of BBC microphones.

From this anarchic mess came *Frankie Howerd Goes East*, a moveable feast of heavy punning and extremely mild innuendo which flowed from Sykes's prolific pen. Against all odds it proved an instant success. BBC bosses may have winced at the often rather 'gappy' pace of the show and radio critics were clearly less than impressed, but the public grasped the point of the disembodied anarchy from the very first broadcast. It was a complete contrast to the staid norm which prevailed on the Light Programme, which pushed the notion that plummy Beeb-speak was the only indication of radio professionalism.

Frankie Howerd Goes East was, even more than his other broadcasts, significantly ahead of its time. Free from the normal constraints, it was a rolling revue that relied almost solely on the sharp wit and talent of Howerd and Sykes.

CHAPTER 6
THIS IS THE MODERN WORLD

Television history books, of which there are many, do not appear to have recorded the significance of 11 January 1952. It was on this date, extraordinarily early in the annals of television history, that the flickery image of Frankie Howerd first appeared on television sets across the country. Not that there were too many – this was still an era when any household boasting a massive, wooden framed television set would see a rather over-regular flow of neighbours, 'just popping in for a peek'.

It is a measure of the then 35-year-old Howerd's popularity that he debuted with his own show, entitled *The Howerd Crowd with the Beverley Sisters*. Noticeably less anarchic than his recent radio exploits, the show sat within the controlled structure of a measured Eric Sykes script that cast a lightly topical mood. (It is interesting to note, in a parallel with television almost fifty years later, that Sykes took great delight in poking fun at the huddle of television chefs who had just started to dominate the early evening programming. Some things never change, it seems.)

In later years Howerd would refer to this debut series with mild though unwarranted embarrassment. True enough, he had yet to learn how to 'project'

In *The Ladykillers* with Alec Guinness, 1955

through the television medium, but it must also be noted that the medium itself was embryonic. Skills in pacing, lighting, make-up and camera presentation had yet to be developed.

'I looked like a pasty-faced village idiot who needed a set of false teeth,' Howerd stated, refusing to acknowledge that this 'village idiot' appearance affected everyone who appeared on television at the time. At least Howerd's nervy delivery remained distinctive, if not idiosyncratic, which is more than can be said of practically any of his small band of television peers, least of all the flour-covered, scone-making cooks with their stilted Beeb speak. Howerd couldn't affect that tone if he tried – two vowels in and he'd fall into his endearing and very camp stutter.

There was a worry, however. From America came the phenomenon of canned laughter: a strange, unfamiliar performance of constructing shows with recording, re-recording, editing, dubbing and finally adding blocks of laughter at a later date. Many people, critics and public alike, initially regarded this as a fraud, if not a downright sham, and it often hilariously seemed so, especially as the same increasingly familiar laughs emerged time and time again.

The idea terrified Howerd. Performing dry, in a camera-filled room devoid of audience warmth, seemed to cast a cloud of inevitability over his television future. Believing himself to be instantly outmoded, a dated variety act, he embarked on a tour of the East – Korea, Hong Kong, Athens, Cairo – for BBC radio, and fully expected to return to a world of over-dubs and forced comedy, which would regard him as an alien. Fortunately, it didn't quite work that way.

His return was pre-empted by a hugely successful television screening of *Frankie Howerd's Korean Concert Party*, which served to bring his radio forces service to the small screen. It proved an extraordinary success and succeeded even in bucking the 'canned laughter' trend. Try as they surely did, the BBC technicians couldn't deny that the show's appeal lay in the link Howerd established with the live audience. To attempt any kind of audience falsifying would have been absurd.

At the London Palladium, still a daunting venue for Howerd, he shone as

Idle Jack in the pantomime *Dick Whittington*. Nevertheless, he would refer to this as, 'The hardest work I ever did in my life. It's one thing performing in front of adults, but attempting to work the sheer unsympathetic honesty of a theatre full of kids is genuinely terrifying. If they don't like you, you're dead. However, if they do like you, then they'll scream the house down – and there's no better feeling in showbiz.'

Howerd's great success with a live audience meant that, far from making him seem outmoded as technology flooded the performance arenas, he developed a certain kudos. The Americans could falsify their celebrities, but Frankie Howerd was the real thing. He was, in the 1952 meaning of the word, hip. When the fearsome theatre critic Kenneth Tynan strongly enthused about Howerd's 'Idle Jack' in the *Sunday Times*, a predictable ripple of other critical endorsements respectfully spread throughout Fleet Street. Howerd's star was now indisputably in the ascendant.

What a pity, therefore, that this critical success was balanced by the professional problems Howerd faced with his agent, Jack Payne: problems that, by the spring of 1953, had turned into an unattractive High Court squabble. Although Howerd would later lay out the points of his argument in his autobiography, and he would genuinely seem to believe his position to be unique, the battle was nothing if not typical of a period where showbiz was learning to work with TV. (Similar battles still happen to this day, of course, when unrest brews between the benign agent, who signs an artist with a career in its infancy and the view of that agent when big money begins to appear.)

In this instance, strong cases were made for both sides of the argument but, after a mess of legal squabbling, the whole thing crashed to a merciful out of court settlement. This freed Howerd but left a barrier between the pair. (Although they would meet at showbiz functions, no words passed between them.) It was a period Howerd found wholly distasteful; although he'd never have sunk ten pints with Jack Payne, he never actually loathed him.

Howerd's way forward was, however, suddenly clear. Changing his former connection with Eric Sykes, he approached a small gaggle of freelance scriptwriters who, with Sykes, slammed down words in a grubby office in Shepherd's Bush. The work generated from that office, a noisy place reverberating with the percussion of typewriters, dense with smoke and swear words, would set Howerd firmly on a path that would lead to *Up Pompeii*. For, in that room, Ray Galton and Alan Simpson worked alongside Sykes. Three enigmatic writing talents who would underpin British television comedy, or at least the best of it, for the next two decades.

It's difficult to sit here now, writing this, and take in that that initial liaison was as early as 1953 – almost twenty years before peak time *Pompeii*. Even then, the reputations in that room were glowing, with Sykes alone having powered the outstanding radio career of the great Tony Hancock, and Howerd's old chum Max Bygraves had also benefited from his work too.

A Galton and Simpson-penned radio series, the somewhat unadventurously titled *The Frankie Howerd Show* (still available in cassette form) proved valuable in keeping Howerd's name afloat. His true excitement, however, was reserved for the oncoming rush of the biggest project of his career to date – a major British comedy film.

It had been on the cards for a while. If anything, Howerd's career had been begging for a filmic interlude for a number of years. Film was (until television took firm control in the early 1960s) still the most natural and esteemed vehicle for any rising comedy talent. It was a magical place to be, and to be seen, the ultimate symbol of success and Howerd, whose earnings were already running staggeringly high – around £600 per week – felt he was floating towards superstardom. Nevertheless the oncoming age of television, which would be Howerd's true vehicle, would be the thing that kept his image homely. Television would create celebrity but not, in the true Hollywood sense, 'stars'. Had Howerd side-stepped television altogether, his household name status would have lessened, but his celebrity might have been more revered, and certainly have a more global appeal.

The film he made was called *The Runaway Bus* and it also starred Margaret

Rutherford and a young Petula Clark who, like Howerd, was a talent simply queuing up for the 1960s television revolution to begin. Simplistic rather than slapstick, it featured Howerd driving a London airport bus in the fog.

There was a little more to it than that, but not much. The bus contained a particularly villainous passenger and everything revolved around the comic possibilities of that scenario: Howerd would later refer fondly to the film as 'a little sketch elongated into absurdity'.

One lovely story, which Howerd recounted on a number of occasions and which also appears in his autobiography, claims that the film, being three minutes too short to qualify for West End screenings, and with only 30 minutes of studio time left, was quickly extended by a scene showing Howerd in a phone box, ad-libbing through a barrage of innuendo.

It worked beautifully. Indeed, the ad libs, which were genuine, even served to provide a little creative *frisson*. It was the perfect opportunity for Howerd to transpose his stand-up talents onto the cinema screen. It allowed him to tease the audience close to him, to set up the kind of cheeky rapport that would soon become his trademark. And to this day the phone box sequence steps boldly from the context of the film.

It is the one snippet where Howerd gains total control. One can almost sense the director's panic and perhaps, imagine the ruinous glares from other members of the cast. Time has fogged any hint of Margaret Rutherford storming from the set. I'm sure she didn't but, in the dour manner that typified her off-screen personality, she would have nodded a begrudging approval. And, though *The Runaway Bus* wasn't Shakespeare, it had a cast worthy of the bard. Howerd is, when you think about it, a classic Shakespearean fool, easily pictured bounding on and off set in *Much Ado About Nothing* or even as *Twelfth Night*'s Malvolio. 'Whenever I see *The Runaway Bus* I find myself creased with embarrassment,' Howerd would later admit, but one senses a certain fondness beneath the statement. If nothing else, the film typifies the era when British cinema flowered in a mess of low-budget self-deprecation.

By now daft things had started to happen to Howerd. Not by accident.

Scriptwriters, directors and producers saw him as a vehicle for modern slapstick absurdity. If there were two ways of doing something, a simple easy way and a difficult, stupid, pointless way, Howerd would choose the latter and stretch it to its limit.

That was his true genius. Howerd would take a joke and stretch it, bend it, wander off at various tangents and lose the plot. All the while the audience would be able to see the easier route. Howerd's craft was the painful art of dismantling something that was working perfectly and rebuilding it in a ramshackle manner. But he'd arrive at a bigger laugh. Why? Because he was Frankie Howerd and he was funny. In much the same way that Tommy Cooper could splutter through some appalling non-gag, sending an audience into stitches for no apparent reason, Howerd could break all the rules of comedy.

A typical example of this indefinable talent came at the very start of *Pardon My French* at the Prince of Wales Theatre where Howerd starred alongside pianist Winifred Atwell. Absurd indeed. Howerd would parachute onto the stage, descending in the manner of Donald Duck, legs swinging in a jerky, fractious descent which ended with him clumping down in an inelegant huddle.

It was quite the most ludicrous thing the audience, or the rest of the cast for that matter, had ever seen. What's more, it takes a special kind of genius to be able to upstage a chorus line of topless showgirls, but somehow Howerd managed to swing it. He brought the house down. He forced a barrage of good reviews and set up *Pardon My French* – a rather mundane romp, to be honest – for a lucrative lengthy spell. High times indeed.

There was a nice postscript to *Pardon My French*. Due to his inelegant excursions, Howerd managed to pull a number of neck muscles and, wonderfully exotic for the time, a masseur was called in to assist him. During the first session, the masseur told Howerd about a friend who wanted to become a comedy scriptwriter. Suppressing a yawn, Howerd told him to bring the friend along, which he duly did. Two days later an impressed Howerd actually purchased a joke from this precocious unknown who went by the name of Johnny Speight. It was 1953. Another giant of 1960s television was

edging into position. Speight would soon be able to give up his job in an insurance office: 'Worst move I ever bloody made,' he once informed Michael Parkinson, in his lovely deadpan manner.

But huge failure was to highlight the spring of 1954. At short notice, Howerd was asked to join the panel on the massively popular Sunday evening television show, *What's My Line?* This was not to be taken lightly. *What's My Line?* commanded almost the entire British television audience. Sunday night was television night. Everyone who had a television sat down and watched it, and, next day, they would tell their less well-off friends what had happened.

Stars could be born overnight. And, of course, destroyed. Howerd's stunted, frozen performance was so incredibly appalling that it actually carried him beyond failure into semi-mythical status. He would cash in on this on the Noël Coward-organized *Night of a Thousand Stars* at the London Palladium. When Howerd was asked a question about getting away from all the bad things in England, he would reply, 'Yes . . . all those things . . . and *What's My Line?*' In an instant he had snatched the sympathy of his audience. His *What's My Line?* failure, although no doubt excruciating for Howerd, had provided him with a vulnerable edge. It was a link with his audience that he would never lose.

In later years, Howerd would reassess what the problem had been and would conclude that he just wasn't cut out for that kind of comedic spontaneity. Although he certainly believed this, it is difficult to agree with him. One thinks of his phone box exploit in *The Runaway Bus*. One thinks also of the countless times on stage where Howerd joyfully drifted from the script and used his sheer force of talent, to carry a gag through a bizarre and complex diversion before returning to his original point.

The truth is that Howerd could take his moveable act to all kinds of extremes providing he felt comfortable with his surroundings. If that was the case he could simply allow the talent to flow. But if something wasn't right, and this something would usually be in his mind, he would implode into a bundle of nerves. His famous nerves would always be the key.

Helping Stanley Holloway celebrate his 65th birthday during filming of *Jumping for Joy*, 1955

'I could never do a Ken Dodd,' Howerd later admitted. 'I may stray from a script if it feels the right thing to do but, to see Ken walking onto a stage and then doing three hours or more without having the entire thing mapped out for him beforehand – well, that is a talent I simply cannot comprehend. I sat through his performance once in a state of complete awe. It was incredibly humbling because I just couldn't see how he could do it. It almost destroyed me but then, one day, Ken told me he felt the same way about me. At first I just thought he was winding me up, but I realized that he meant it. It was only then that I realized that it – comedy – that it comes from somewhere else. It's pointless trying to define it and it's pointless for someone like me to copy someone like Ken. I believe he is a genius and I am an idiot. But he doesn't see it that way.'

The above statement is pulled from a truly anarchic five-minute slot in the middle of an early 1970s *Granada Reports* (a magazine news show for the north-west of England). During the slot, in which Howerd was asked to talk about Liverpool, he left the hapless interviewer – could have been Bill Grundy or, more probably, Bob Greaves – spluttering in off-camera confusion as he decided, at the last minute, to use the slot to champion Ken Dodd. It was a small and, in the scheme of things, rather insignificant piece of local television. However, these weren't the antics of a man who felt 'uncomfortable' with ad-libbing on live television.

CHAPTER 7
DOWN AND OUT IN JUAN LES PINS

Away from spotlight and microphone, Howerd was not the kind of fumbling self-obsessed character one might expect. At times he was a curious opposite of his public persona. Given his image of bumbling campness, his gossipy ranting and savage self-deprecation, it's easy to imagine him surrounded by toadying sycophants, holding forth in some showbiz bar on the brink of Soho, or some shabbily genteel club in St James's.

But it was not so. In private, Howerd emerged as a reasonably complete and confident character. Friends remember him kicking a football around Hyde Park, which is a surprising image. In his autobiography he admits to being a 'fair tennis player', which is apparently true. And far from holing up in his flat, devouring scripts and consumed by rampant ambition, Howerd was a regular sight walking his dog, Red, through London parks, enjoying the air, chatting amiably to anyone who would dare to approach. Not at all the curmudgeon of showbiz folklore.

He was also a passionate reader of books about the tradition and history of theatre. Theatrical biographies were an obvious choice as he looked for things to relate to. But he also avidly devoured 'in-house' publications such as the *History of the Prince of Wales Theatre*.

He wasn't a great one for holidays but, in the Britain of 1954, a holiday usually meant little more than a damp fortnight in Fleetwood. Famously, however, he visited exotic Juan les Pins on the French Riviera during these years, where he was stunned to discover that his personal wealth, considerable by English standards, seemed rather pathetic in comparison to the ostentation that surrounded him in Nice.

'I was with a girlfriend and my sister Betty and her friend,' he recalled. 'We were just awestruck tourists. I adored the heat and the yachts and the buildings and the food and the money. I pondered on this a month later when I was sitting in a dank hotel in Nottingham. Suddenly it dawned on me that my life wasn't quite as glamorous I had previously thought. I came down to earth.'

Literally. In Nottingham, during a run of, rather ironically, *Pardon My French*, Howerd tumbled down a flight of stairs in full view of the audience and painfully snapped an ankle. The audience roared with laughter, demanding more wonderful timing from this master of slapstick. Howerd smiled as he retreated to hospital. The run would continue, with Howerd prising as many laughs as humanly possible from a pair of crutches and a plaster cast.

In June 1955 came the second series of BBC TV's *The Howerd Crowd*. Simplistic in format, this one-hour show was, yet again, forged from a barrage of Eric Sykes gags. Although the show was regarded as a success, and certainly kept Howerd implanted in the minds of the general public, the star was uncomfortably aware that television light entertainment was being pulled towards the fringes of the rock'n'roll revolution. Almost overnight a host of new pop stars, all clean-cut, asexual copies of the American originals, were beginning to assemble on the side of the TV stage.

The transformation of these new singers from spirited youths fronting precocious bands to glittery showbiz acts really did happen in an instant, and Howerd felt seriously threatened by the emergence of Tommy Steele, Cliff Richard and Adam Faith as all-round family entertainers. His fears were only partly justified. We now know that idiosyncratic comedic talents would be in demand for the next fifty years at least, and perhaps Howerd should have been

more wary of the progress made by his old friend Benny Hill, who, remarkable as it may seem, had already debuted *The Benny Hill Show* on the BBC by the summer of 1955.

Howerd, concerned about being usurped by the rock rollercoaster, decided to concentrate more on acting. A second film, *Jumping for Joy*, saw him embroiled in comic adventures at White City dog track. Less successful than *The Runaway Bus*, it is a curiously awkward affair. Howerd's performance was acceptable enough, but the public's imagination wasn't captured.

Despite the film's obvious shortcomings, Howerd found himself plunged into a crisis, obsessively determined to emerge as a comic actor rather than a television comedian. It's a classic situation. At heart, he desired greater credibility and a more heavyweight public persona, to become a comic actor rather than a mere television celebrity. Whether this was, as he would later suggest, a period where he had started to take himself a little too seriously remains in doubt. Whatever the reasons, he fell into an artistic confusion which was to be swiftly followed by a ferocious attack of self-doubt. As Howerd plumbed the depths of despair, fortune intervened at a most appropriate moment. In a move that would push him further down the road to attaining comic actor status, he was offered a part in another film. Called *A Touch of the Sun,* it was, much to Howerd's astonishment, to be filmed in Juan les Pins. A return to the Côte d'Azur was too good an opportunity to miss and, as he booked into his hotel room, it must have seemed as though he was, at last, soaking in some genuine filmstar-style glamour.

'It was unreal,' he exclaimed. 'I was sitting in cafés looking out to the Med, chatting to Alfie Bass. Yes, well, you can't have everything.' It was probably the time he spent on location that made Howerd decide to pursue his acting dream, rather than the film itself, which, although quite appealing in a lightweight, holidayish kind of way, fared even less well than *Jumping for Joy*.

Not that the decision would prove immediately correct. Two months later he would turn down the chance to top the bill at a West End revue in order to concentrate on what he regarded as, 'The more serious business of acting.'

Perhaps Howerd sensed that this was a wrong decision when his replacement in the review at the Prince of Wales, Dickie Henderson, became an immediate and acclaimed success. It was 1957 and Howerd, dislodged, confused and exhausted, retreated into the English countryside for a period of relaxation and self-scrutiny. For four weeks he banned himself from reading newspapers – lest, no doubt, he would stumble across rave reviews of Dickie Henderson – and did little more than hobble around the country lanes of Dorset, stopping occasionally for a lunchtime drink in some refreshingly lazy pub.

Although his friends were concerned, and one newspaper had made ludicrous claims that Howerd was in a state of 'nervous breakdown', the countryside break was a wise and necessary opt out of a career whose pace had been building for several years. When he finally returned to London, he was focused, and all the more determined to pursue his acting dream.

Refreshed and still ambitious, Frankie Howerd threw himself into the noble profession. He would, indeed, be an 'aack-tooor', albeit a snivelling one of the comic variety, full of mildly bawdy witticisms. In retrospect we might well say that it didn't matter a jot what Frankie Howerd was doing: the fact was, Frankie Howerd would always be Frankie Howerd, and no amount of thespian pretension would ever be able to change that.

This was proved by his dubious choice to slot into the place left by the departing Alec Guinness in a then-touring French farce, *Hotel Paradiso*. Unfortunately the new billing seemed to attract only Howerd fans, all wanting him to stumble and wince, roll his eyes and winge. Which is exactly what they got. With Guinness the role had been given a refined air. With Howerd it became a performance of common banter.

Howerd tells a nice story in his autobiography about his time on tour with *Hotel Paradiso*. In Bristol he was introduced to a gangly chap named Peter O'Toole, whom he befriended and took to dinner. 'You'll make it big in six years,' he told the handsome though all-too-often rather inebriated young buck. 'Trust me to get it all wrong,' grimaced Howerd in retrospect. 'Within two years, he was a superstar.'

A Shakespearean exploit followed *Paradiso* with Howerd's unexpected appearance as Bottom in *A Midsummer Night's Dream*. Although Howerd owned a Shakespearean face, he never claimed to really understand the plays, but Bottom suited him. It is a foolish part which begs interpretation and, although Howerd struggled with the language, he still made the role in his own manner that, to some, seemed disrespectfully anarchic and to others refreshingly innovative. In truth, it was neither. It was just Frankie bumbling gloriously along. The notices in the daily press were, to say the least, mixed.

Yet, Howerd's credibility rose. He wasn't convinced about it, himself, but he really had succeeded in deepening his image. A television appearance in Molière's *The School for Wives*, in which he portrayed a craggy sex-starved, sixty-year-old, failed, however, to improve on this new public perception of him. The fact was that the television audience just wasn't ready for Molière. And they still aren't.

Howerd knew it was not necessarily a bad thing that Molière was not as popular as *Sunday Night at the London Palladium*. His cosy appeal could only be lessened by a mass audience seeing him as a misanthropic backbiter. No, a little thespian credibility was one thing, but meddling with the power of celebrity, even in 1957, was a dangerous business.

With Danny la Rue on *The Frankie Howerd Show*
Overleaf: In *A Touch of the Sun* with Dennis Price, 1956

CHAPTER 8
VENUS AND SCARBOROUGH

Mercifully, Howerd didn't have time to sit and ponder. In Manchester, at the Opera House, he starred in an extraordinary musical called *Mr Venus* which had initially been written for Norman Wisdom. It was a clever tale, too clever perhaps for the time, being about an alien visitor arriving on earth with a mission to preach the power of love. Unable to communicate the message, he chose a lowly bar worker – Frankie Howerd – as his unwilling medium. It was not a bad idea at all and certainly one brimming with comedic potential. Unfortunately, the production department was somewhat lacking – the show had no director and no one to organize the music, nor anyone to shift and sort the complex scenery.

These may seem rather obvious omissions but, to Howerd's horror, it soon became apparent that his show was tumbling towards its premier with most of the cast simply not knowing what they were supposed to do. Worse still was the situation backstage. Normally a show is built on the confidence the actors gain from the rock-like professionalism of the supporting technicians. With days rather than weeks to the first night, the show was a confused mess.

For example, the alien costume arrived and when worn, transformed the dignified actor Anton Diffring into a cross between a Christmas tree fairy and

As Buttons in *Cinderella* at the Streatham Hill Theatre

something that, two decades later, might be playing saxophone in Earth, Wind and Fire. Then a day before opening, it became apparent that the set designer had been working to different timings than the actors, so the scenery just didn't match the scene. The whole thing was rapidly degenerating into farce. Howerd spent the night before the opening sitting in the corner of The Grapes public house, just around the corner from the Opera House and frequented by Manchester's impressive pre-1960s glitterati.

He had been worried about this play from the outset, to the point of suggesting that his part be taken by his friend Max Bygraves, but he had no idea that such terrifying backstage anarchy would ensue. Stumbling out of the pub, too worried to be inebriated, Frankie and the rest of the cast returned to the theatre and worked through the night to get some sense of order. It was hopeless. They managed to pace and place the first half of the show but, as dawn broke over Deansgate, the cast had no alternative but to scamper to their beds. The next day rushed at them like a train through a tunnel. They managed

to scramble through the first half. It wasn't going to attract rave reviews but it just about made it to the interval. The second half must have been one of the most incredible hours in the history of the Opera House. For, as the audience moved from mild bemusement to irritable grumbling, to near violence, then apathy and mass exodus, before all these changing moods, a bewildering swirl of ad-libs, falling scenery, falling dancers, truncated songs, blank silent spaces and nervous prompts took place. It might have been mesmerizing, had the audience had some prior notion that they were to witness the theatrical equivalent of freeform jazz. All rules would break down and only twelve members of the audience, by all accounts, actually survived to the end. If Howerd had had his way, he would have presented them with some kind of official honour.

Incredibly, *Mr Venus* survived this first night. By the time it reached Liverpool it had even been blessed with a director, Eleanor Fazan, who stripped it down to the bare bones before painstakingly piecing it all back together. To the delight and amazement of the cast, the hurried new format did appear to make some kind of sense. Even so, Howerd was stunned when he received a note from the Prince of Wales Theatre, which still seemed keen to stage the show. As the tour stumbled through the provinces and much to the consternation of original writer Alan Melville, heavyweight comic writers Eric Sykes, Johnny Speight and Galton and Simpson were drafted in to transform the entire affair into a Howerd showpiece. The plot was duly twisted until the plot of the love-sharing alien was crushed and a battery of jokes turned the entire thing into a comedy love farce.

It wasn't good, either. Perhaps they should have worked with the chaos of the second half, and transformed that into a new production – a play within a play? – rather than rewrite the whole affair. It ran for less than three weeks. Indeed, it crashed to a heartbreaking end on the Saturday night before Howerd

From left to right: Frankie Howerd, Lionel Jeffries and David Tomlinson in *Further Up the Creek,* 1958 appeared on *Sunday Night at the London Palladium*. Although his stand-up routine had been polished to perfection, he was still wallowing in post-show sadness and he delivered, in his own words, 'the driest, dullest, greyest piece of entertaining ever to take place on that hallowed stage'. Undoubtedly an exaggeration but, nevertheless, Howerd's star had slipped and even the kindness displayed by London's bundle of theatre critics couldn't disguise the fact that he was in grave danger of becoming an act of the 50s. A radio act. A pre-rock'n'roll fade-out. The new age had arrived; and had Frankie Howerd, with his craggy comic face and his camp English delivery, become passé?

It certainly seemed that way. There was an old-time aura around Frankie Howerd and it refused to go away. More radio work with Johnny Speight followed which, surprisingly, failed to stimulate either audience or press. Speight, still some years from *Till Death Us Do Part*, was himself attracting charges of being plain old hat, just a radio man. Ironic to say the least, since he would go on to help invent the notion of peak time sitcom satire and, arguably, become the most significant British television comedy writer of the 1960s.

Hurt and depressed, Howerd once again retreated from the scene, spending time horse-riding in the Brecon Beacons. As unlucky as ever, this seemingly innocuous break resulted in calamity as Howerd found himself rolling down a Welsh mountainside, bruising himself all over and smashing his wrist. The *Daily Sketch* covered the story and, in an exaggeration of late 1980s tabloid proportions, pronounced Howerd to be in a state of 'near death'. He was nothing of the sort. Indeed, he regarded himself as incredibly fortunate to have escaped with such minor injuries.

In his autobiography, Howerd regards this period not just as a lull but as a black hole during which he was no longer a star. This wasn't true at all, and even that *Daily Sketch* silliness should have offered him proof that his name commanded interest. What actually happened was that Howerd himself, injured by his trail of comparative failure, had started to think that he had fallen from celebrity grace. He'd wander streets, in Gloucester, Cirencester and London, convinced that nobody recognized him. He believed himself to be in

With Warren Mitchell in *The Frankie Howerd Show*

the shadows. A dangerous position from which, given the influx of new performers, he quite possibly might never re-emerge.

Although this obscurity was an illusion, it would eventually be regarded as a positive thing. It certainly instilled a new hunger in him as a performer. He would, he told himself, bounce back with a vengeance. And so he would – in the unlikely environs of Scarborough.

Scarborough in the late 1950s was a typical bustling British holiday resort. In later years, as working-class Britain was tempted to sunnier climates, it would attain a tea room quaintness and remain profoundly time-warped, locked in the late 1950s, when it first gained a young, fashionable edge. Howerd loved Scarborough from the outset. With its clean air and enchanting display of pastel colours, it was soundtracked by seagulls and, on the prom, transistors blaring the new rock'n'roll. Teddy boys patrolled the ice cream parlours, injecting menace into the atmosphere, but Howerd didn't care. It was a different universe. London lay somewhere else entirely. He felt he could fail in Scarborough and nobody would notice. However, that wouldn't happen. He had arrived at the town intent on just one thing; becoming a big fish in a small pond. He might not be a celebrity on Wardour Street but, in such a holiday town, his star would shine again. He was determined not only to snowball his career, but to reinvent himself as a kindly man of the people.

On the prom he would smile and sign autographs for little old ladies. It would be an easy show, and, during his time off, he would relax, eat ice cream and not worry about reviews or agents or anything beyond the confines of this rather sweet seaside resort. In true Howerd fashion, the little nirvana in his head would fail to materialize and a rather darker reality took over. Scarborough, unlikely as it may seem, sizzled beneath a relentless sun for almost the entire season. Great news, of course, for the town's tourist board but tragic for any theatrical production. With the best will in the world, who would want to spend three hours sitting in a dark theatre during such weather?

Not even Howerd, it seemed.

'I couldn't blame anyone for not coming to the show,' he recalled. 'The truth was that it was sheer hell being in that theatre knowing how glorious it was outside. You'd have had to be insane to go in there. Fortunately, there were a few such lunatics.'

The show was a rather bland revue in which Howerd was allowed to work through a series of sketches, refining them as he went along and, as it turned out, softening them considerably to suit the rather more conservative theatrical climes of Scarborough. Even so, after a fortnight, it was suggested to him that he 'tone down his act a little'. This threw him into confusion. Since 'toning down' his act was, or so he believed, exactly what he had been doing for two shows a day, six days a week.

His act involved sauntering onto the stage as if he had just wandered off the beach which, on some occasions, wasn't far from the truth. From that base, dressed like a particularly naff seasiding Englishman, and exuding anti-glamour, he could easily fall into a tirade of self-deprecation. Pure, simple Howerd, adapting to his surroundings. Following the management's curious objections, he pulled out a sketch he'd previously employed in *Dick Whittington* which saw him as a little boy who, having left his semi-licked lollipop on a park bench, attempts to get it back despite the bench being used by a courting couple. The act was an elastic mime, allowing Howerd to stretch it any way that suited and making full use of his extreme facial expressions. It was also about as bawdy as TV cook Fanny Craddock. Less so, now I come to think of it. Nevertheless, the notion of a courting couple was seen as hard-core pornography by the management, who shackled the comic in a bout of unprecedented censorship. When Howerd later recalled these events in his autobiography, he referred to the theatre's manager as 'Thing'. Twenty years later, as he wrote, he was still seething.

Truly, it must have been dispiriting. His Scarborough dream was transforming into a nightmare and there was nothing he could do about it. Every time he plucked a new joke from the depths of his memory, the manager knocked it back. Towards the end of the run, Howerd's act had been chopped and changed into what was, he felt, little more than an unworkable chunk of tepid blandness. Although he still loved the town, and would escape onto the majestic north York moors at every opportunity, the memories of that summer season would remain as an unsettling shadow. The 1960s were clicking into gear, the world was already rocking with venom, the television industry was revving with intent – and Frankie Howerd was walking, alone, on the moors of Yorkshire, lost in obscurity, thoroughly convinced that his star had finally flickered to nothing.

Somewhat bizarrely, perhaps seeking an antithesis, Howerd flew to New York. He needed, he felt, the scramble of a big city, the allure of truly big-time showbiz and New York, more than London, was establishing itself as the very heart of the new era of rock'n'roll-tinged showbiz. That said, he was amazed at the archaic television techniques used in *The Ed Sullivan Show*, filmed live in an old theatre. For three weeks he fluttered around the New York glitterati and, heartbreakingly, just failed to land a dream role in a Broadway revue starring Hermione Gingold who, Howerd was stunned to discover, was a fan of his. Cruelly, however, just as Howerd's hopes started to soar and he could see the headlines about how this English comic may have failed in Scarborough but had subsequently taken America by storm, just as this new dream seemed possible, the chance was viciously snatched away, leaving him alone in the most competitive showbiz environment on earth.

Returning to London he surprised himself by securing a prime spot in the television panto, *Mother Goose*, where his 'Dame' immediately grabbed the necessary warm revues. 'Frankie Howerd was crazed and captivating,' wrote the *Daily Sketch* and, despite the slight back-handed tone of that sentence, it was to be the most welcome notice of his career. He was surprised to discover that, while walking on Wardour Street, a number of kindly folk recognized him. As naive as it may sound, he really didn't realize that his television status hadn't necessarily been altered by his time in the wilds of Yorkshire. Indeed, with repeat transmissions, nobody had even noticed his disappearance. For the first time in his life he saw that television stardom, indeed *any* stardom, works in a separate time zone. Yes, it can fade in an instant but, conversely, it can elongate a star's dominance.

Courageously considering his *What's My Line?* experiences, Howerd allowed himself to be cajoled into the new television production of *Twenty Questions*, which had enjoyed a lengthy and highly successful run on radio, pretty much typifying British radio at the heart of the twentieth century. But would it work on television? And for Frankie Howerd, could he manage to get over those *What's My Line?* jitters? The producer, Maurice Winnick, a man of considerable perception, still believed that Howerd's personality could work and evolve in such a tight television situation. On a panel, surrounded by fast minds – Muriel Young, Stuart McPherson, Stephen Potter – Howerd could inject a necessary pathos.

Howerd would later talk down the show, which didn't work as well as it had on radio. Something about radio to this day drags the listener close to such a panel while, on television, the very same team can appear self-congratulatory and egotistical. Nevertheless, *Twenty Questions* wasn't quite the disaster that Howerd believed. Not only did it keep his face in the living rooms of Britain, ushering him into the next decade, but it set a template for an endless string of shows with similar formats which still continues to this day. From *Twenty Questions* to *It's Only TV But I Like It* and dozens of other celebrity quiz shows isn't very far at all.

Helping to create innovative television might have kept his face familiar to the nation but it didn't necessarily pay the bills. Whatever money he managed to save was inevitably snatched by the tax man, who was all too happy to disbelieve the relatively small earnings of a big star. Although Howerd had enjoyed periods when he earned considerable amounts of money, he had also learned the old freelance truth, that the good times never seem to stretch across the sparse times. He was living in Holland Park. Not the Holland Park of today, where media people munch rocket salad lunches at £50 a throw, but the mixed, unfashionable and comparatively shabby Holland Park of the early 1960s. Even swapping his rented flat for a mortgaged mews house didn't seem to improve matters. Too often he would wander alone in Hyde Park, still seriously wondering whether the showbiz life really would sustain him through the normal expanse of a career.

Later he would hint that this, yet another dark age no better than the Scarborough of the previous year, brought with it a virtual nervous breakdown, although there is no evidence that things quite went that far. Surprisingly, perhaps, he did attend church – alone, always alone – and would sit praying silently, such was the extent of his desperation. It was 1960 and, although his face was still there on TV, his period of 'rest' started to stretch dangerously from weeks to months.

This hiatus would have lasted for years had it not been for a brief spell as Buttons in *Cinderella* at the Streatham Hill Theatre. It was a low-budget production and rather a long way from the Broadway debut of his dreams, but it was work and, albeit eventually, it would lead to a string of tentative offers. It was difficult, though, to shake off the aura of 'has-been' that seemed to hover nastily around his name. Not to the public, who still hadn't noticed his low-key existence, but to the London posse of agents who were striding hopefully into the brave new media-aware era of the 1960s. Wasn't Frankie Howerd a creature from a fading era? It was the same old problem. He was offered bit parts, cameos, small chinks of showbiz light. He knew only too well that he could easily turn into a dinosaur, a gimmick, a mere flashback.

Paradoxically, and probably because of his 'flashback' status, he was invited onto the panel of the pop review programme *Juke Box Jury*. It was absurd, for Howerd was always, and would remain, on the flip side of rock'n'roll. He loathed pop music, aside from the songs delivered by friends like Max Bygraves. Nevertheless, he bumbled his way entertainingly through the show and the absurdity of his appearance – 'What can one say about Adam Faith?' he mumbled, adding, 'Oooh I don't know. I wonder if he has ever considered singing?' – seemed to gain him a small measure of cult status. This may not have meant much in 1960, but it was better than nothing. It was enough to trigger a lengthy feature on him in the *Sunday Pictorial*, which homed in on his existential forays to Yorkshire and New York. It was enough also to hoist him onto the new screening of *Sunday Night at the London Palladium*, albeit at the 'wrong' end of the bill.

Then, still in the doldrums, he accepted a chance to work with Tommy Steele, one of the brightest of the toothy Brit pop stars at Great Yarmouth. That might not sound too exciting but Great Yarmouth was a large and burgeoning resort – a resort stacked with stars. Bruce Forsyth! Bob Monkhouse! Max Bygraves! Frankie Howerd! Suddenly it felt as though he'd re-entered the fray. His season at Yarmouth was short and sweet, which only made his trip back to unwelcoming London something of an anticlimax.

With Sid James (left) and Michael Kilgarriff in *Puss in Boots* at the Coventry Theatre

CHAPTER 9
THE ESTABLISHMENT

Frankie Howerd was still in a state of flux. His early taste of fame had twisted his expectations and left him floundering. He was caught between stardom and unemployment, extremely aware that his celebrity status didn't come with any guarantees. He still had great friends within the industry, a whole stack of them who seemed to be engrossed in multitudinous work offers, he still had a public who seemed to genuinely love him, but he felt like a fading star. Unfortunately for him, the London agents continued to spread the myth: Howerd had cooled. His phone rarely trilled.

In 1962, with The Beatles breaking everywhere, Frankie Howerd decided to quit showbiz. He'd had three years on a downward spiral, with pockets of work punctuating months of self-pitying stagnation. In one courageous attempt to break from the rigors of television and pantomime, he came terrifyingly close to buying his own tiny night club. More reasonably, he took time to seriously consider running a pub. He even went through the motions of contacting breweries and, while appearing in panto at Southsea, visited a few potential hostelries. It would have been an interesting pub, no mistake about that. One can see a line of locals at the bar, soaking in the anecdotes delivered by their celebrity landlord. He was serious, though. He saw this as an ideal method of wrenching himself away from his misery. As an indication of just how bizarre the spectrum of his choice had become, it might be noted that while Howerd was looking over pubs in Eltham, he was simultaneously being seriously considered for the part of Fagin in the Broadway version of Lionel Bart's *Oliver!* He didn't get the part: producer Dave Merrick believed Howerd wasn't evil enough, and perhaps he was right. Merrick couldn't have known it, but his knock-back came very close to condemning one of the great comic talents of the last century to the role of pub landlord.

And then, suddenly, events transpired to dramatically shift the landscape of his life. There was great sadness with the death of his mother, who always believed Howerd would become a huge star. Then, just one day later, he received an invitation to appear on Alma Cogan's *Star Time* show on ITV. It took Howerd by complete surprise, for it was the first such offer he had received in some time. His appearance kick-started a roll of events that would carry him back into of being one of the 'happening' acts in Britain.

'It was peculiar,' he later told the BBC's Brian Redhead, 'because I really had totally given up at that point. I know everyone says that, and if it had happened a month earlier I couldn't say such a thing, but I had reached the point of no return and then, with my mother dying, something snapped. I'd gone. And just at that point, something reached out and pulled me straight back in. Life is funny sometimes.' More television, this time in the noisy form of a *Billy Cotton Band* television special, was immediately followed by a glorious radio series. It was specifically written to showcase Howerd's talents, and the writers, Marty Feldman and Barry Took, were working at the height of their powers.

Enter Winner – Michael Winner, self-styled cinematic genius and socialite – who grasped Howerd by the collar and persuaded him to play the lead role in his bizarre new film *The Cool Mikado*, a syncopated and thoroughly appalling version of the Gilbert and Sullivan classic. Well, it's a classic if you like that kind of thing. Howerd didn't, as it happened, but he was drawn towards the idea of working in the new British avant garde. It certainly made a change from Scarborough. Even if the film would gain cult status as one of the worst pieces of pretentious drivel ever produced at Shepperton Studios, it still helped propel Howerd back into the limelight. And back into the centre of things. Circulating around him now were a whole host of talented newcomers. Mike and Bernie Winters, Tommy Cooper and Pete Murray all cowered beneath the daft despotism of Winner, who would later admit that, during this period, he 'lost it, rather'. Clearly Winner was attempting a cinematic Picasso and falling into a hideous trap of taking himself far too seriously. It was, in part, the making of a man who would go on to enjoy fantastic success pushing low art films for the mainstream audience.

The Cool Mikado became a running joke between Howerd and Winner. Indeed, it became a running joke between any two people who ever saw it. Howerd's performance, as Koko, is certainly one of the most extraordinary things this writer has ever seen. None of the cast had any idea what the film was about or how it related to the original. Even after it was released as the low point of double features across the country, they remained none the wiser.

Immediately following this entertaining madness, Peter Cook asked Howerd to appear at the recently-established Establishment Club, which had been instigated by himself, Dudley Moore and Jonathan Miller in the wake of their legendary *Beyond the Fringe* success. It was an honour that seemed all the more profound when Howerd discovered he was to appear at the infamous venue the night after Lenny Bruce! With this in mind, and aware of the fact that to blow it would send him spinning back to pub landlord vacancies, Howerd contacted Johnny Speight and together they began working on a satirical act that would suit Howerd's talents.

As Johnny Speight recalled, in conversation with Russell Harty in 1985, 'It was very odd because Britain had just latched onto satire and producers were screaming for "the new comedy", as they called it. What was strange was that all the agents and producers were regarding Frankie as "old school" but none

of the new generation of comedians or writers saw him that way at all. In fact, we saw him as the perfect vehicle. He could read anything and make it funny, even pretentious in-jokes about the government. Nobody who knew what they were talking about was at all surprised when Frankie made it really big. Down at the Establishment he used a few satirical jokes but they weren't really topical the way he did them. He was incredibly, er, reactionary? So *out* that he was in. People just loved him and that cut across all kinds of barriers.'

Howerd's ability to appeal to the new generation of comic audiences was itself a precursor for post-Python times, when 'old school' comics such as Tommy Cooper, Les Dawson and Morecambe and Wise would often, to their own bemusement, gain strong cult followings among audiences more naturally attracted to the young, sharp and hip. The thing is, no matter which way you analyse it, Tommy Cooper is funnier than Alexei Sayle.

With the help of the Establishment and, following on from his appearances there, Ned Sherrin's hugely innovative *That Was The Week That Was*, Frankie Howerd was suddenly hip! He really was. One indication of this came via the *Evening Standard* Drama Awards which, to his utter amazement, honoured him for 'Services to the Theatre'. He was, for once, speechless. (Actually, that's not strictly true. He did have a speech in his pocket but, far from being words of acceptance, it was a speech written praising all those who had so deservedly won on this prestigious occasion.) Arguably, Frankie Howerd was the only star in the history of awards ceremonies who was genuinely rendered agog, mystified by his success. On the podium, such as it was thirty-six years before All Saints at the Brits and Gwyneth Paltrow at the Oscars, Frankie Howerd broke down and cried. Another first! His life was changing fast and would continue to do so when, within weeks, something unexpected would again occur to catapult him into comedic immortality.

The Cool Mikado, 1962

CHAPTER 10
A FUNNY THING . . .

It began in America. A little whirlwind of a show, skimming around Broadway, gathering extraordinary notices. It was daft, camp, completely at odds with anything else. It owed more to British pantomime than American revue. It was loosely scripted and bawdy. It shouldn't have worked at all, but it did.

It was called *A Funny Thing Happened on the Way to the Forum*. A musical romp written by the young Stephen Sondheim (book by Larry Gelbart and Burt Shevelore), who'd won acclaim as a collaborator with Leonard Bernstein on *West Side Story* but had yet to succeed on his own, it was so out of step with everything else on Broadway at the time that absolutely everyone was talking about it. For over a year the show had won acclaim in New York and it was inevitable that there would be a London version. When the West End show was finally anounced, it was no less a thespian legend than John Gielgud who put forward the name of 'Frankie Howerd' as its star.

'The show was pure Frankie without Frankie knowing about it,' he stated. 'I don't know whether, in some weird way, he had initially influenced it, there is no evidence for that. But I wouldn't be at all surprised. And when (producers) Hal Prince and Richard Pilbrow asked me if I knew who could play the

In A Funny Thing Happened on the Way to the Forum with Kenneth Connor

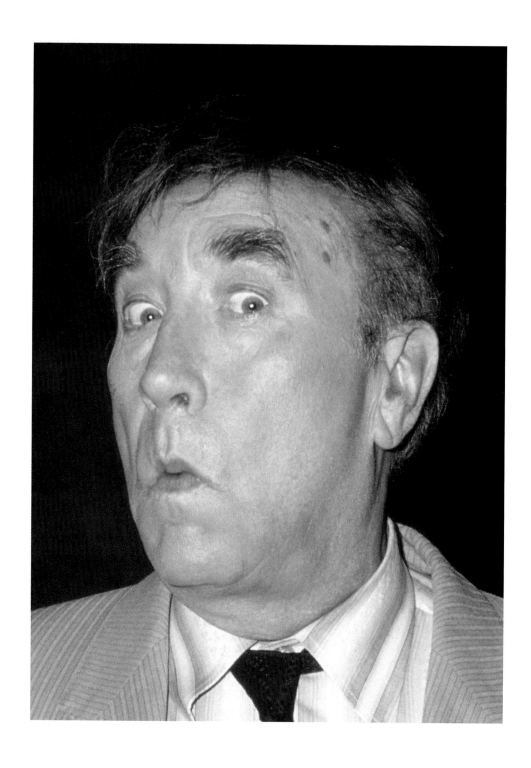

London lead, well there was only one name in my mind.'

The writers of *A Funny Thing . . .* , Sondheim and Gelbart, duly turned up to catch Howerd in *Puss in Boots* at Coventry. Which in itself was bizarre. These were two Americans – profoundly American by all accounts – and they'd surely never seen anything remotely like an English pantomime before. Howerd would later admit, in his autobiography, to being absolutely terrified before that particular performance. How could they grasp *Puss in Boots*? Well, perhaps their lack of exposure to British panto helped. They saw a show dripping with ferocious anarchy and with a script, stupid to begin with, that warped this way and that according to the reactions of the crowd – and what a crowd. Two thousand manic infants! They were more than merely enthused, they left Coventry spellbound, partly by the general absurdity and partly by the way that Frankie Howerd wandered amid such madness and seemed completely at home. It was indeed unlike anything they had ever seen and, in their minds, they had found their star.

Backstage that night, as the crazed hordes departed, Frankie Howerd was offered the role of Pseudolus. However, worried that Howerd's reputation for 'script warping' would soften their punch lines, they resolutely demanded that, should he accept the part, he wouldn't be allowed to tamper. He didn't care. He agreed there and then.

The phone rang. And again. And again. And again. Now it was becoming annoying. The silence of the preceding years had been broken. 'Friends' came out of the shadows. Agents called him. He was repeatedly invited to lunch. His name was dropped all over London, at every showbiz party, at every first night. Television offers crowded for his attention – radio, too. Everybody, it seemed, wanted a part of Frankie Howerd.

He was at once delighted and infuriated. The superficiality of his world had never seemed so glaringly obvious. The love that apparently now flowed towards him was never so hollow. The offers, though welcome and the more the merrier, were soaked in falsification. Ah well . . . so be it. Better than sitting alone on the north York moor. Better than Scarborough. Although, curiously, it didn't seem better at the time. Part of Frankie Howerd yearned for the simplicity that goes with failure. Walking along Scarborough prom, wallowing in misery . . . well, it now seemed strangely attractive. Such is the paradox of success. Still, up to this point it had all been rumour and gossip. Messing around in Coventry panto was one thing. Frankie Howerd now had the West End within his grasp and it was up to him to take this chance and transform it into something real and lasting. Something of genuine worth. Which is exactly what he did. It was a busy time. With everyone who, just a month ago, had claimed he was washed up now wanting a piece of him, he found that, for the first time in his life, he could afford to be choosy. He took risks – great risks. Relying heavily on the talents of Galton and Simpson, Barry Took, Dennis Norden and Johnny Speight (the very heart of British comedy writing), Howerd threw himself into a particularly memorable *That Was The Week That Was* in which he tore Reginald Maudling's Budget to pieces in typical fashion. While performers with a more natural eye for satire, in particular David Frost, seemed to struggle to lighten the weight of Budget news, Howerd simply stole the show. Ironically, he would have been successful without any script at all. He could have mumbled, have thrown in a few 'ooohs' and 'aaahs' and still taken the honours. It had nothing whatsoever to do with matters satirical, but it was great fun. What's more, the press agreed.

'Nobody knows quite why Frankie Howerd was on *That Was The Week That Was*,' claimed the *Daily Mirror*, sagely adding, 'but everyone was glad he was there. It was Howerd alone who lightened a miserable night's viewing.' Presumably the remainder of the evening was taken up by dry-as-dust Budget news, with Frankie Howerd as the lone antidote.

In Manchester, under the guidance of DJ Dave Lee Travis and with Paul McCartney calling into his dressing room, Frankie Howerd opened the Mr Smith's night club on Whitworth Street. In retrospect, this might not seem particularly prestigious, but in fact it was. Manchester in 1963 was widely regarded as the nightclub capital of Europe – although in reality it had faded a little since its 1950s heyday. It was, with Liverpool, the heart of Merseybeat and Mr Smith's was widely expected to carry on the legacy left by the fading Oasis and Three Coins, the two city's main R'n'B venues of the city. It did exactly that, fronting a scene that was shaping towards mid-1960s discos and, more notably, extraordinary soul clubs like The Twisted Wheel. In short, the pre-George Best set Manchester 'in crowd' would all be in dutiful attendance – hip young soul mods and modettes. Howerd was bemused. His *That Was The Week That Was* appearance had conferred upon him an unexpected credibility. These kids loved him. More importantly though, they were happy to be seen loving him. Shortly afterwards, Howerd flew to New York to catch *A Funny Thing Happened on the Way to the Forum*. He was stunned by what he saw. He adored it, but remained unsure whether he would be suited to it.

Nevertheless, while performing through the summer in Jersey, Howerd spent each morning munching toast, slurping coffee and delving through the script. He was particularly attracted to the 'lightness' of the writing. The script, as such, mattered little. It was a vehicle for a string of gags and absurd situations. These were linked by a complex and brilliant Sondheim score, which Howerd took time to learn by heart. Not the most natural singer in the world, which is why he initially thought Bygraves would be better suited, he was still able to inject enough personality into his voice to just about carry a tune. Working with a full orchestra would still present a heavy challenge, though, and Frankie would later refer to this period of learning as, 'quite the hardest work I had ever done'.

He sensed that he was on the verge of something really important. He knew the successes of the previous twelve months would crumble away if he couldn't find a way to consolidate them. It had happened to him once before; this time around, he was determined to seize the opportunity. He never wanted to be wandering, hurt and alone, again. Jersey provided him with a perfect base in which to work and relax. He adored the tiny island, its infamous 'chumminess'

With (from left to right) Anita Harris, Hattie Jacques and June Jago in *Carry On Doctor*, 1967

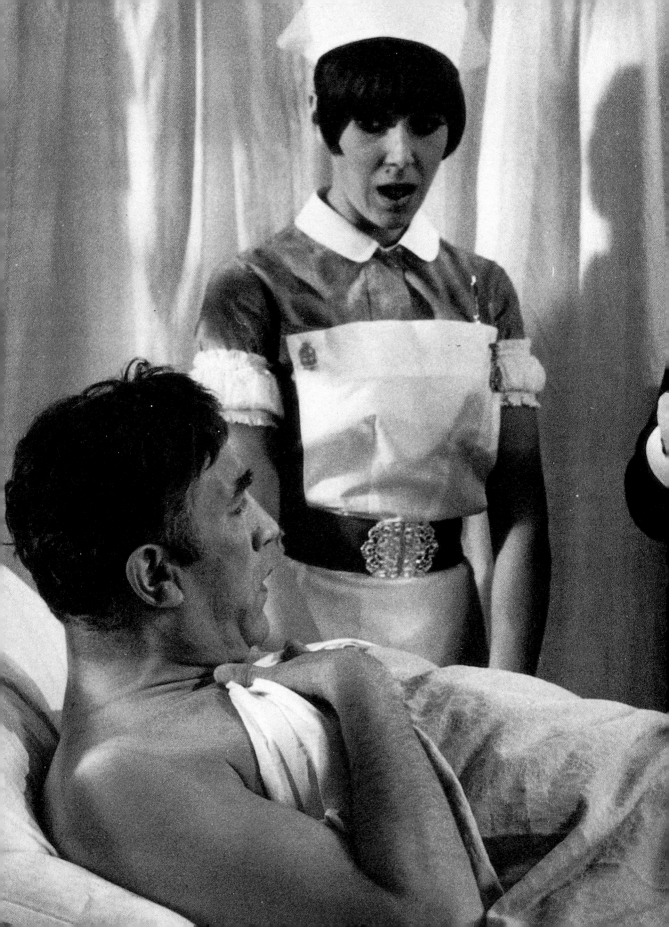

and the curious feeling that it is 'not quite like anywhere else on Earth'. Celebrity had an unusual definition in Jersey, for the island was, and remains, stocked with vacationing celebs. Within the context of the island, however, they remained generally unpestered, simply accepted into the swing of things. 'I never thought about getting recognized in Jersey,' he recalled in the *Observer* magazine in 1988. 'I know I did, especially by holidaymakers, but somehow such things seem more relaxed over there. It made me feel normal, which was definitely a good thing because, in London at that time, my head had been getting a bit big.' To his credit, Howerd was always ready to recognize the fact that celebrity, as a state of mind, was dangerous, shallow and ultimately pointless. It was the work that mattered above all else.

There was a nice little incident which indicates just how high his particular celebrity star had risen in 1963. While in Jersey, the Beatles, who had exploded across the globe in a manner never seen before or since, asked if they could catch his show. The theatre owner grumbled about allocating four free tickets as the show was fully sold out, and his naiveté in not realizing the kudos granted to his little theatre by allowing the hottest pop group in the world through his doors seemed to mirror the prevailing Jersey attitude. It was exactly why Howerd found it so easy to relax there. He was almost reluctant to return to England, where a serious bout of work awaited. *A Funny Thing . . .* had been simmering on the back boiler for too long. Solid rehearsals kept Howerd closeted but, by the time the show stuttered around the provinces for a pre West End try-out, the laughs were clearly in place.

The show opened in London on 3 October 1963, to good but not glowing reviews. If they were a disappointment, Howerd was too busy to notice. (As it turned out, critical opinion gradually began to rise. *A Funny Thing . . .* ran until July 1965 – a fantastic achievement.) Frankie Howerd would later admit that, come opening night in London, he was petrified. The publicist working the show had done a job that was, in effect, too good. The hype had been bubbling away for weeks, laying a huge burden on the shoulders of all the cast, especially Howerd who, naturally, couldn't help but think back to the traumatic time of *Mr Venus*. As the lead, he had to carry the entire show on his shoulders. Indeed, during the lengthy performance he was only allowed offstage for three minutes. Enough time to sling down a glass of water and to allow the nerves to build, which was something of a relief. Co-stars Kenneth Connor, Jon Pertwee, Robertson Hare and Eddie Gray would all build careers from the base of *Forum*.

Seconds before curtain-up Howerd, resplendent in the kind of toga that would soon become his trademark, froze and started complaining bitterly to George Giles, one of the four actors playing eunuchs during the opening scene. It is to Giles's credit that he refused to bow to his leading man's plea for help, and sent Howerd trundling to the front of the stage with a flea in his ear. Howerd would later thank Giles for cutting his stage fright dead in an instant, thereby setting up the show. 'If it hadn't been for that incident,' Howerd later confessed, '*Forum* might never have got off the ground and my entire career would have fallen away.'

It was, undoubtedly, the most important night of his life.

Frankie Howerd would always refer to *Forum* as a 'happy show'. It was happy because it was a success, because the cast all grew comfortable with it and, most of all, because its star had truly found his niche. To go and see the show would be to see an integral part of mid-1960s London theatre. It was one of those shows that seemed to epitomize the entire decade. The changes that occurred within modern culture between October 1963 and July 1965 were simply unprecedented – for the Beatles alone, from the simple 'She Loves You' to the complex *Revolver*. From blast-hard beat groups to psychedelia. Hair had grown, lapels widened, trousers flared, flowers had attached themselves to shirts and jeans. Young, streetwise political thought had hurtled towards the revolutionary left and London had entered its most evocative age of glamour since the 1920s. Hairdressers and photographers were among the new stars. Carnaby Street was a colourful strip and had yet to sink into nausea-inducing tackiness. Mods stopped fighting rockers. Students, when not rioting, were preaching the benefits of peace. Marijuana had replaced Purple Hearts. Joss

sticks burned at parties. And if you spent more than five minutes in Leicester Square, someone would thrust a flyer into your hand inviting you to go and see *A Funny Thing Happened on the Way to the Forum*. If you were an American tourist, or down from Manchester for a two-day break, enjoying a West End honeymoon, or simply there for a week's business, you would go and see the show. It was part of a London that felt like the cultural centre of the world. *Forum* would burn the name Frankie Howerd into that fantastic era. It would provide him with a certain immortality.

Two-and-a-half frantic years at the Strand Theatre. Two shows daily. Long, arduous performances – and still there were television appearances – *Sunday Night at the London Palladium* – even two fabulous Galton and Simpson-scripted television series during the course of 1964. By this time, the writing team understood the Howerd character to perfection and had him delivering monologues written in a manner that allowed him to elongate them and add his own touches. Often they would prompt him into action by leaving the script dangling precariously so that Howerd would fill the gaps with his usual remarks or rather non-remarks: 'Ooohlookmadam . . .Oh, she's so common!'

Howerd's Beatles connection should have been cemented with a cameo appearance in *Help!,* second of The Fabs' daft but loveable romps. Both of which have stood the test of time, perhaps because, rather than being mere promos for their new selection of songs, the daftness within both films was a pretty accurate reflection of the band's celebrated sense of comic camaraderie. Howerd, invited onto the film, was fascinated by this and by the sheer absurdity of having to arrive, each day, at a studio absolutely besieged with squealing teenage girls. Surging through an ambuscade of Beatlemania every morning proved genuinely dangerous. 'They would hurl themselves at anyone who looked as though they might vaguely be connected with the Beatles. It was certainly bewildering for me,' he recalled.

More bewildering still was the fact that Howerd's on-camera antics never

Left: Programme for *A Funny Thing. . .*

Overleaf: with Joan Sims and Sid James in *Carry On Up the Jungle,* 1969

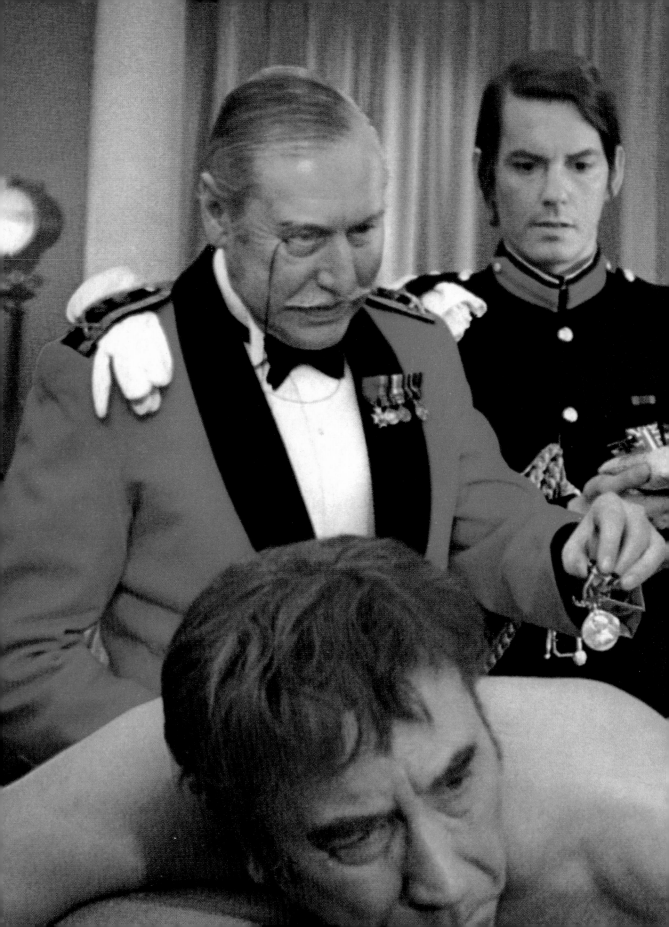

Previous page: A familiar pose from *Up the Front*, 1972

made it to the final cut. There has never been any explanation for this. Howerd liked to believe that the lads didn't want to be upstaged, but it was almost certainly nothing more sinister than hasty and perhaps rather clumsy editing.

At the final curtain of Howerd's *Forum*, the comic fell happily out of his work schedule utterly exhausted but, this time, positively buzzing with contentment. Perversely, he then opted to depart for Borneo in another of his 'entertain the troops' escapades. Nobody in British showbiz could quite understand why he went, but clearly, building unpredictability into his career proved not to be a bad thing. It was a Howerdian trait, to arrive at a place of comfort, fame and relative wealth only to skip off to an uncomfortable climate, and one where such fame meant very little indeed.

CHAPTER 11
SNAKES AND LADDERS

Frankie Howerd went to Gan and then Malaya and while there lost sight of the Eastern paradise around him, seeing only the creepy-crawlies for which he developed a wholly understandable fear; snakes, rats and spiders the size of hands. Then there was the boiling heat. And all the time, the BBC crew followed Howerd and his little gang from gig to gig, taking the hot, bad-tempered comedian out to buy fruit from the markets, to wander along idyllic beaches and among cattle loose in the villages. Though it hinted that Howerd was living this fantastic, glamorous, country-hopping life, the reality was nothing but painful, with Howerd working hard at the shows, then allowing himself to be filmed while apparently relaxing, which is not relaxing at all.

In Borneo, Howerd was helicoptered into dense jungle where his act and accompanying documentary, *East of Howerd,* was punctuated by the terrifying shrieks and cries of the jungle. It did seem a touch bizarre. Performing before a steamy array of Nissen huts and sweating squaddies might have looked glamorous and gallant on the BBC but Howerd had repeatedly to remind himself why he was doing this. The problem was, that he couldn't actually come up with any reason at all.

'I suppose I took some comfort from the fact that I was genuinely bringing a little bit of cheer to the lives of soldiers who were living in pretty miserable circumstances,' he later recalled. 'It was worthwhile for that reason and because it served to remind me how superficial and unimportant the showbiz life really was. It was humbling. I was humbled . . . oh, how I was humbled.' There's another sweet example of Howerd's talent. That line, delivered during a BBC radio broadcast in the late 1970s (with Harry Secombe on *The Comedy Route*) isn't remotely funny in print but, delivered with the exact amount of Howerdian pathos – I've played it over and over again – it's curiously hilarious. Why? I have absolutely no idea. Howerd seemed to be parodying the tactic often used by patronizing showbiz celebs affecting the 'Oh I'm so insignificant' approach (while meaning exactly the opposite, of course) but, with Howerd, it seemed possible to believe him. He had built into his comic stutter a genuine humility. Others may argue against that, of course: occasional autograph hunters possibly shunned when they lunged at him as he was leaving the London Palladium, perhaps. Such stories abound and they have, to some extent, damaged his reputation. But such stories are exaggerated and easily countered by examples of opposite behaviour. While never exactly being Howerd the approachable, he could be genuinely courteous. What's more, despite being enveloped by his mid-1960s stardom, one strongly senses that he never lost sight of the absurdity of it all. If he had then, frankly, he wouldn't have been so funny.

Perverse as ever, Howerd chose to follow his nightmare trip to the East with a nightmare trip to the West – to America and Mexico. Not, this time, with any intention of working, but to relax. Naturally such a notion proved impossible. Could Frankie Howerd ever relax? Possibly, when reading a historical biography, but not on a frantic trip zipping to and fro across the North

American continent. In his autobiography Howerd tells of his strange and sudden fear of flying, something he had never felt before and which, possibly, could have come about as a result of his helicopter trips in Borneo. Whatever the reason, it meant that his American experience was dulled by a numbing over-indulgence in alcohol and tranquillizers. Whether it was the side effects of his chemical intake or not will never be known, but Howerd would often refer to the night in a Mexican village when, following a thunderstorm, he encountered a thirty-foot snake. You could tell by his delivery that he wasn't entirely convinced the snake was real but, even if it was hallucinated, it would produce a shudder of terror in him for the rest of his life.

'I'm terrified of snakes,' he told Michael Parkinson. 'But for a while they seemed to be following me around the world.' They didn't follow him home, though, and at the close of 1965 Frankie Howerd found his true cinematic level when he was given the lead in Frank Launder's *The Great St Trinian's Train Robbery* playing opposite the superb Dora Bryan. Filming involved a great deal of jumping on and off trains and chucking eggs around. It was to prove a real joy, both to make and to watch.

The film was a light confection – gleeful, cheekily English and resolutely old-fashioned. Its frantic pacing and anarchic script perfectly suited Howerd and Bryan and, to this day, when it flickers into view, usually on wet Saturday afternoons or on Tuesdays when you are recovering from 'flu, it never fails to cheer the spirit. Certainly, it was the film that finally banished bad memories of *A Cool Mikado*. It's interesting to note that, in the psychedelic year of 1966, *The Great St Trinian's Train Robbery* – which was nothing more than a cheeky nod towards the real Great Train Robbery still so embedded in the nation's psyche – was one of the most popular films. Arts writers, casting critical nods back to the era, rarely mention this fact. What a pity. Personally, I find it to be a far more vivid and profound glimpse of a lost era than some over-stylized, clumsy, psychedelic hotch-potch slapped together by (usually) a pretentious bearded geek carrying his fat ego on his shoulder. But that's merely to voice an unpopular opinion. Give me a saucy giggle any day.

In the spring of 1966 came BBC TV's Galton and Simpson-scripted *The Frankie Howerd Show*, which might be regarded as the pivotal series of his entire career. For here he was, in a splattering of simplistic sketches, doing nothing particularly challenging. Nothing that – the cleverness of the script aside – really stretched the bounds of mid-1960s mainstream television. And yet it still seemed strangely extraordinary. Americans visiting England would have gazed in utter bewilderment and exclaimed, 'Just what the hell is thaaat?' Even though the format would be almost identical to multitudinous American shows of the time.

But Howerd could take that straight, mainstream format and twist it in his eccentric English way. Around this time he was asked to star in the Eric Sykes-directed revue *Way Out in Piccadilly* at the Prince of Wales Theatre, a show which also boasted the tentative West End debut of Cilla Black. The pairing was intriguing – Howerd the battle-weary craggy comic pitched against Black, a pop star whose Liverpudlian exuberance was pushing her toward a long and rewarding TV career. It could have been disastrous, but in fact they got along perfectly. Black, feeling her way, entrusted herself to Howerd's greater experience and the comic, in return, admired the professionalism and eagerness of this disarmingly straightforward girl. It was a combination that proved so successful that the show ran for a solid twelve months, picking up an impressive collection of excellent notices along the way. Black would later claim it to be the most rewarding experience of her career and, without doubt, the skills she learned during that period would provide her with a grounding in the mainstream showbiz arena. Eric Sykes, noting the speed at which she learned, and in front of a live audience at that, would help further her television career by guiding her towards the right producers.

The show, plus an extraordinary Royal Variety Performance that year, helped Howerd earn the honour of 'Showbusiness Personality of the Year' for 1966, presented in February 1967, by the Variety Club of Great Britain. It is a strong indication that, during this period, Howerd's career was truly peaking. Naturally, his work rate increased to dangerous levels. Imagine working on the

Carry On, Doctor feature film while simultaneously recording a TV spectacular for Christmas, two radio shows and at the same time constantly skimming through television and film scripts seemingly written entirely around the Howerd persona. That, perhaps more than anything else, was the highest accolade of all to Frankie Howerd. Aspiring writers now saw him as the rock on which they might build their careers. It was a compliment, without doubt, but it brought with it a great deal of pressure. 'Mr Howerd, would you read my script, I've spent two years writing it especially for you. Please do it as my entire career depends on it.' This was the kind of thing that confronted Howerd at every turn.

'I was beginning to get a reputation as a work horse and the problem was that people were expecting me to say yes to everything,' he later recalled. 'It was just ridiculous. Of course, I was very flattered and it was a fantastic position to be in, but I was never very good at saying no. I had to employ other people to do that. And then people started thinking that I was stand-offish. I wasn't. But I was getting tired.' That tiredness was a contributing factor to a serious bout of pneumonia that kept Howerd from his work commitments during 1967. Immediately on recovery he was lucky enough to be given a large part in the exceptional pre-*Blazing Saddles* Western-style spoof, *The Wind in the Sassafras Tree*, a play which opened at the Belgrade Theatre in Coventry, to sensational notices: 'Howerd's performance is sublime, at last he has found a play that is as ludicrous as he is.'

That may seem a trifle back-handed, but Howerd didn't mind. He loved hearing stories of irate London agents who had wanted the play for themselves. (They hadn't, actually. Several of them had turned it down. Funny how their attitude changed the instant they saw the reviews.) But the show was spoiled by the appalling decision to take it straight to America, by-passing London's West End. Without the experience gained by a good solid West End run, there was no way of judging quite how the Americans would perceive it. Or, more importantly, how the American theatre critics would see it. Nothing in England can compare with the power that critics in cities such as Washington, Chicago and New York could, and still can, wield. These people could strangle a play at birth – especially a play that pokes fun at an American invention, the Western. Westerns were often absurd – full of Brylcreemed, clean-cut cowboys shooting scruffy evil Injuns. Still, Americans took offence, despite Howerd naturally stretching the lines to the absolute limit in his lovely British style.

The initial reviews for this genuinely funny play were the most vicious Howerd had ever encountered, and he became public enemy number one. 'I took over from the communists,' he later joked, although he was clearly hurt by the experience. Despite initially lukewarm reviews, though, theatregoers were beginning to warm to the show and word was starting to get around that it was well worth viewing. And then one powerful critic, Clive Barnes of *The New York Times*, slammed it and it was finished. The entire show crashed to a halt. Howerd was stunned. Not at the review but at the extraordinary power of that one notice, isolated as it was, in a pool of reviews that were beginning to sense that the show could be a hit. But in New York, the hardest theatre area in the world in which to create a hit show – Howerd said that only one in thirty-six shows manage to stay open, though the reality is more like one in sixty-six – *The Wind in the Sassafras Tree* instantly became nothing more than another also-ran.

Back in London, with a hole in his diary and still irritable about the treatment he received in America, Howerd was immediately requested to top the bill at the Royal Variety Show when Eric Morecambe withdrew following a minor heart attack. Before the announcement of Howerd's booking, the newspapers carried countless stories of speculation. The question of who would be Morecombe's replacement put Howerd at the centre of a minor media storm. Who could hone an act in just fourteen days, asked the papers. The list of possibles wasn't that long, to be honest, and the public perhaps didn't quite care as much as the press believed, but it was a harmless enough angle. Who could it be? An American – Bob Hope? Sammy Davis Jnr? Could it be Sinatra? Hardly the kind of speculation guaranteed to calm a comic's nerves. Especially as one name resolutely missing from that list was Frankie

Howerd. 'Whoever it is, expect something special!' screamed the *Daily Mirror*. Pressure? What pressure?

And it would continue to grow as everyone involved at the Variety Show suddenly latched onto the fact that, as a publicity device, this speculation was absolutely ideal. What's more, if it could be kept a secret right up until the moment of appearance, all the better! What finer way of ensuring that the tension remained intact until the show's final flourish? What a marvellous piece of publicity! What an enormous weight on the shoulders of poor Frankie! By the evening of the show, people were expecting a performer of at least God-like stature. Judy Garland would have struggled to deliver under such pressure.

Howerd found relief in the instructions that he was not to enter the theatre until moments before his appearance, lest the secret be allowed to buzz through the audience during the show. Well, at least that would prevent him from succumbing to the mounting tension that always grew backstage at this particular event and, as previously mentioned, had caused some of the greatest and most experienced stars in the world to melt.

So Howerd hovered around Soho that night, running his routine through his head time and again, unhindered by the tension in the Palladium. The second to last act was Diana Ross and The Supremes, surging through a triumphant 'Baby Love' while the expectant crowd watched with suspense. Who could the next act be?

At last, in stark contrast to the American pop beat, came the strains of 'Land of Hope and Glory'. A good tactic. Playing to the patriotism of the occasion. It would obviously be an English performer. On strode Howerd. He stopped, turned centre stage and faced the audience. And for one split second . . . the longest of Howerd's life . . . nothing happened. Then came spontaneous applause. Relief surged through the theatre and Howerd both. He visibly relaxed into a masterful, apparently effortless performance. Two factors worked in Howerd's favour. Firstly, the British audience knew all about Howerd's American flop. As such the 'Land of Hope and Glory' theme which brushed away the Supremes' snare-beat was a clear winner. Secondly,

Howerd's on-stage reference to Eric Morecambe – a genuine reference, one could never doubt – caught the audience's sympathy.

It was a winner. It might be noted, for nothing other than personal, insular and pretty dull reasons that affect only the person writing this book, that Howerd's first public appearance following this evening of great and mighty glory was at the Poco á Poco Club in Stockport. Such are the swings and roundabouts of showbiz. With respect to working men's clubs in, oh, I don't know, Rotherham or somewhere equally dreadful who might like to claim this honour, it must be noted that the Poco á Poco was quite simply the darkest, dankest, most profoundly unglamorous cabaret venue on the entire planet. Perched on the edge of undemanding Reddish, the Poco á Poco was the place where people who couldn't be bothered to trek into Manchester would go. A crumbling ex-cinema, the Poco á Poco provided a rather different challenge for visiting celebrities. Frankie Howerd never quite forgot that engagement.

'I've played some dives in my time . . . but I needed an aqualung that night,' he quipped. I'd like to say, as someone who visited the venue on a regular basis (though not, sadly, on that night): on behalf of Stockport – sorry! Still, rather like Borneo, it served to keep him humble. The Poco á Poco night was filmed by a local Granada Television crew who had filmed a local rock'n'roller called Rockin' Tome the previous week. A shaky, strangely lit film remains. It shows Howerd striding around the stage as if searching for the exit while sending nervy witticisms into the darkened hole that, presumably, held an audience.

Later that year, Frankie Howerd was to get married. On film, that is. To Joan Sims in *Carry On Up the Jungle* which, though not in the class of *St Trinian's,* was bouncy enough to enjoy a reasonable amount of success. The chemistry between Howerd and Sims was, as he would state in *On the Way I Lost It*, profoundly, hilariously asexual. As such, the marriage scene held an added edge. Watch it now and you will see both of them hovering on the brink of breaking into hysterics. It's a marvellous moment – and apparently genuine – that goes somewhat towards making up for a film that, despite the promise of its title, must rank as one of the more lacklustre *Carry On*'s.

CHAPTER 12
AND SO TO POMPEII

With *Carry On Up the Jungle,* a link had been forged. Script writer Talbot Rothwell had been working on a severe rejig of *A Funny Thing Happened on the Way to the Forum.* The rejig had become increasingly serious and increasingly angled toward Howerd. Rothwell had worked it up and up and up until, finally convinced that he had uprooted something very special indeed, he approached Howerd himself.

The background to *Up Pompeii* is somehow typically English. The BBC's Head of Comedy, Michael Mills, had been away on holiday in Italy and while there had made a visit to the ruins of Pompeii. When wandering amid the area that had been full of bordellos and shops, so goes the legend, he had suddenly turned to his friend, Tom Sloan and exclaimed, 'This place is amazing. I keep expecting to see Frankie Howerd come loping round the corner.' His thoughts were obviously flashing back to *A Funny Thing Happened on the Way to the Forum* and so, on returning home, he dug out a copy of the plays of Plautus and sent them to Rothwell along with a note that read, 'What about this for Frankie Howerd?' Rothwell loved the idea and, dropping several pressing projects, set to work. It is interesting to note that many of the plays of Plautus feature a slave bouncing around the set, organizing the whole show to his

With Shirley Eaton and Lance Percival in *Up Pompeii*, 1971

specific advantage. That character did surface in *Forum* too, but the Mills/Rothwell idea was to take the character – by now called Lurcio – just a little further.

When Howerd read the script he knew immediately. No doubt about it. With the dubious background of pagan Rome to lean on, the opportunities for absurd innuendo were simply limitless. Daft, corny gags would gel with effortless ease. Written specifically for Howerd, Rothwell's embryonic script simply begged for Howerdisms. Howerd was ecstatic – his only reservation being the possibility that, because it was designed to head straight onto television rather than begin life in the cinema or theatre, it might be rather too bawdy for the living rooms of Britain.

It was a genuine concern, although there was something paradoxical about the apparent cleanliness of television in the late 1960s/early 1970s. Although you wouldn't get anything like the Channel 5 boob fests of today, some of the lines that had been aired during series like *The Lovers* and later, *Man About the House* would raise a few eyebrows even today. My theory, for what it's worth, is that we never quite understood just how rude some of those lines were. Of course, bawdiness is more than just allowed in Britain. In some parts of the country it's demanded and is actually part of the tradition of the many seaside resorts which line the island's coast. There's a direct line from the fool at the royal court of Henry VIII to naughty seaside postcards and music hall innuendo.

But, yes, there was a concern. At Howerd's request a pilot show was made. To his delight Mary Whitehouse, the patronizing, self-elected arbiter of good taste and decency, was absolutely furious and couldn't understand how Howerd could lower himself in such a way. The great British public were rather more intelligent than that and, following rave notices, certainly expressed a desire to see more.

Howerd's own appraisal offered in *On the Way I Lost It* described the programme as 'a send-up of sex: demonstrating that obsession with it is silly and ludicrous'. If Mary Whitehouse had any sense at all she would have understood that people were quite capable of deciphering that for themselves. The pilot was repeated twice and continued to catch growing audiences. There was absolutely no way that the BBC would pass on such a hit; the thirst for low-brow music hall silliness, the odd flash of cleavage and odd bum joke was so obviously great. For the first series of six shows the format was whittled down to basics. Howerd's Lurcio sat and addressed the camera with a hilarious narrative blessed with an obvious sense of fake outrage. The method was astonishing. A bad joke – the cornier the better – would serve only to set up Howerd's self-righteous indignation. Hence: 'What's a Grecian urn?' 'A hundred drachmas a day.' General groans. Lurcio: 'Look, it may be old to you but it was brand new in 54 AD . . . Oooh, please yourselves.'

The idea was to drag the viewers into Lurcio's inner circle. Hence the wonderfully chummy dialogue. Lurcio: 'Greetings noble citizens, simple plebeians, crafty artisans and arty courtesans . . . I think that about covers the lot . . . now let's get straight to the fruity part . . . '

Like *Fawlty Towers,* it is always a surprise to discover just how few episodes of *Up Pompeii* were actually made – just fourteen, spread over two series. However, they were repeated so often and the scripts were so refreshingly loose that no one ever really noticed the differences from week to week, or that it was the very same series they had so attentively watched only six months previously, such was the show's easy allure.

For a full five years at the start of the 1970s, it really did seem as if, come 9pm, Frankie Howerd would pop up in a toga. Which he did. Again and again and again and again. The impression was that Howerd was doing nothing else but *Up Pompeii*. It had, for him at least, an unsettling effect. His public, television persona became quite separate from him while he carried on, beavering away in the background, eventually unable to compete with a character he'd personally left behind years before. 'It was the only time in my life when I seriously started to wonder if I had created something that would

Overleaf: Being held by Rita Webb, the soothsayer, in *Up Pompeii,* 1971

eventually turn against me,' he later said, although such fears were unjustified. Lurcio was loveable, mischievous, Machiavellian perhaps, but ultimately of little resonance.

That said, *Up Pompeii* swept around the world and, in great anarchic style, actively changed the rather po-faced stance of numerous television channels, particularly in the staid areas of New Zealand, Australia and Canada where, until falling for Lurcio's dubious charm, people had never before encountered anything similar before. After *Pompeii*, however, production teams of numerous nationalities started making numerous low-budget shows full of cheap laughs.

With the television series a resounding success, it was time to take Lurcio onto the cinema screen. This proved relatively easy as Talbot Rothwell still seemed to have more to build into the character and his scripting of the first film, *Up Pompeii*, not only kept the character alive but expanded the social setting accordingly. It would prove to be the best of three *Pompeii* films, partly because Rothwell was so adept at using the medium to the full – it was the only one of the films that didn't seem to be just an elongated version of the television show – and partly because Galton and Simpson, who wrote *Up the Chastity Belt*, never quite, for all their brilliance, grasped the heart of Lurcio. Which was fair enough since he wasn't their creation.

Chastity Belt, produced by Ned Sherrin, also suffered from savage editing and flirts too rapidly around a tight circle of innuendo. The finished product, although ironically outperforming the first film at the box office, had a claustrophobic feel and Howerd never seemed particularly comfortable. He would later admit that the second film displeased him. Reading Howerd's comments, on radio and in print – he touches upon it in his autobiography – one can sense a growing tension between him and Sherrin who, rather contrary to his amiable radio image, was apparently something of a despot on set, chastizing Howerd for arriving late and forcing him to read from scripts that the star felt were a little awkward. The same tension seemed to spoil the third film, *Up the Front* (also directed by Sherrin), which at least enjoyed an expanded, starry cast including Zsa Zsa Gabor, Stanley Holloway and Dora Bryan. Howerd tells a good story about Sherrin reluctantly allowing him a morning off so the star could recover from Liz Taylor's fortieth birthday bash, in Budapest.

That particular bash was one of the most famously star-studded gatherings in major celeb history. It's almost a shame that *Hello,* and *OK!* magazines weren't around to capture it in all its lavish glory. For better or worse, it reflected an era when stars were shiningly charismatic, shamelessly wealthy and more than happy to flaunt it and somehow, somehow manage to retain the love of a large section of the public. (Posh and Becks wouldn't have made it past the car park attendant.) The resultant hangover and predictable airport delays caused Howerd to return to the *Up the Front* set in a state of red-eyed exhaustion. Sherrin slapped him straight back into action and, I swear this is true, you can see him doddering drunkenly about on the finished cut. Not that it particularly mattered. As Howerd would say, it wasn't *The Godfather*. Sherrin, however, appeared to treat it as such. Alas, the tension didn't act as a spark and the opposite was in fact true. *Up the Front* remains interesting because of the amount of celebrity involved but for little else. One simple fact was clear: *Up Pompeii* was only really *Up Pompeii* when Talbot Rothwell was involved.

Nevertheless, *Up the Front* did signal that Howerd was no longer a lonely, frightened Brit splashing around in the major celebrity league. The film, dubious as it was, inflated his fame in, of all places, America, a country that had never been particularly fond of him (a feeling that was wholeheartedly mutual). But Howerd's bad feelings toward America were somewhat tempered on a visit to Los Angeles to promote *Up the Front*. He stayed at the Château Marmont off Sunset Strip, and enjoyed the full force of major league showbiz glamour by being invited round to Bob Hope's mushroom-shaped home on a hill overlooking the idyllic desert playground known as Palm Springs. He got

In *Up the Chastity Belt*, 1971, with Eartha Kitt

on well with Hope – who, of course, made great play of the fact that they were both born in Eltham.

In 1972, the BBC requested a third series of *Up Pompeii*, despite Howerd's protestations that the show was becoming too staid and familiar. As it turned out, Talbot Rothwell's health had deteriorated to such an extent that he was unable to work. The new series was, therefore, rendered impossible, for no other writer could have taken on that particular mantle. It was Rothwell's signature and it couldn't be imitated. At least not on television, where the intimacy between Lurcio and the viewers was at its most effective.

Rothwell's health would continue to deteriorate and, sadly, he would die in 1981 from a heart condition in a Worthing hospital. Many were surprised to discover that he was only 64. The BBC, to their credit, decided not to force the issue despite a few insensitive mumblings. 'Would the public really notice?' they asked, but Howerd, along with most people involved in the production, was resolute. The only solution, it seemed, was to drum up a similar series, one that would maintain the level of historical farce, offer that barrage of innuendo and retain the fondness that had developed between Lurcio and the audience.

The result was *Whoops Baghdad* or, more specifically, *Frankie Howerd in Whoops Baghdad*. It was a strangely disjointed affair and the quality varied tremendously from episode to episode. Howerd played Ali Oopla, the bondservant to the Wazir of Baghdad, played by Derek Francis. Six half-hour episodes were produced; they drifted quietly onto the screens in the middle of 1973 and it was immediately apparent that the chemistry of *Pompeii* was sadly lacking. There were a number of obvious problems. A mini conveyor belt of writers with clashing ideas about Oopla's character served only to muddle the identity of the central figure. Lurcio had been easy to latch onto: Ali Oopla wasn't as distinctive or indeed as funny. There were also problems in the background. Producer John Howerd Davies found Howerd 'difficult'. And he probably was, for Howerd's confidence in the script resulted in him questioning everything, from the set design – which was never as funny as the gloriously 'naff' *Pompeii* set – to the surrounding cast, who struggled to work with Howerd's increasingly unpredictable 'attack'. Filmed before a live audience, Howerd would often ad-lib in their direction at the expense of a cast member. For example, after a particularly clumsy scene with a beautiful actress, he turned to the audience to confide, 'Ooooh, she was dreadful . . . You see what I have to put up with.' This wasn't, I suggest, quite as cruel as it now seems in print, for he was only employing his celebrated panto technique to inject some spirit into the show. Still, it didn't help his burgeoning reputation for awkwardness.

The series was boosted by a succession of risqué trailers which not only featured girls in extreme states of undress, but were shunted out during 'Children's Hour' even though the series itself wasn't shown until after 10pm. This dubious tactic resulted in *Whoops Baghdad* attracting a cult following, not least with the confused thirteen-year-old schoolboys of 1973. The message was that *Whoops Baghdad* was likely to be somewhat harder, somewhat ruder than *Pompeii* – and it was therefore certainly worth conning your parents into letting you stay up for it. Alas, expectations raised by the trailers were not matched by either fun or frolics on the screen. *Baghdad* wasn't without its sexual attractions, but it completely failed to back them up with the necessary requisite sense of anarchy.

One critic described it as 'Howerd Gone Limp' which perhaps justifies the star's temperamental attitude towards the series. It wasn't, incidentally, a flop – BBC figures suggest its audience was similar to *Pompeii*. Its impact, though, was considerably smaller.

CHAPTER 13
HOLLYWOOD AND BEYOND

Few people believed that Howerd would be able to make any serious headway
in Hollywood. He was, it was often said, 'too English, too *Carry On*'. The
irony of this was that, should you ask any Hollywood comic of the time to
name the best English comedian, more often than not Howerd would be the
first on their lips. Bob Hope, in particular, was always quick to lavish praise on
our bewildered star. There was something about Howerd that, against the
prevailing wisdom, actually did seem to translate. While in Hollywood, where
he was languishing more and more – though the thought of Frankie Howerd
drifting along Sunset Boulevard or soaking in the sun on the beaches of Malibu
remains difficult to imagine – he was presented with a number of film scripts.
This, in itself, is not so surprising; film scripts circulate like worthless
counterfeit dollars in LA, only one in a thousand apparently carrying any
genuine promise. However, Howerd was drawn towards one particular
treatment, a comedy thriller entitled *The House in Nightmare Park* in which
the role of a Victorian ham actor was seemingly written with him in mind.
He accepted it.

The film was duly made and gained a good deal of critical praise. It was a
bombastic Gothic romp, basically. Nothing to particularly set Hollywood

ablaze, but certainly good enough to turn a few Hollywood heads towards the possibilities of this unusually weathered comedian who seemed to be blessed with filmic potential. However, Howerd would use the film – or rather the filming – as a rich source of anecdote for his interviews, both on television and in print. One of the most intriguing aspects of this was that Howerd, to his utter terror, had to perform in certain situations that would normally be handed over to a stunt double. 'Perhaps they just couldn't find a stuntman who looked like me,' he later quipped, which may not have been too far from the truth – not many Frankie Howerd lookalikes tend to hang around the bars of Pacific Palisades. In one astonishing scene, Howerd had to relax against a door which suddenly splintered as an axe crashed through. The fact that the axe was real and that Howerd had to do three takes while a nurse hovered nearby would provide him with a number of comedic angles for future interviews. There was also the small problem of the scene in which he had to stand in a pit full of snakes. 'Well, it won't be too bad, just me and a few plastic snakes,' Howerd famously remarked. 'It's a bit more *elaborate* than that,' replied director Peter Sykes. 'Just how *elaborate* is it?' asked Howerd.

It is a pity, really, that such background traumas couldn't have been included in the finished film. Needless to say, 'elaborate' meant that Howerd would be filming in a pit with dozens of real snakes. No acting necessary. The scene was good, and it's not difficult to sense a genuine streak of terror in the actor. Howerd would later curiously explain to Michael Parkinson that, 'For a while I felt quite close to the snakes. They weren't horrible creatures at all.'

More standard Howerdian adventure awaited back in London where he starred as Simple Simon in *Jack and the Beanstalk* at the London Palladium, arguably the country's top panto production. It was Howerd's first pantomime for a decade and he could be forgiven for forgetting just how exhausting such shows can be. For three months he lived in a darkened netherworld of backstage corridors, hardly having time to nip home to sleep let alone reserving space for a social life. Mostly he stayed with the cast who, to his delight, included Dora Bryan and Alfie Bass. It was a pleasurable enclave of old time

British comedy. It is one of the curiosities of pantomime (or, at least it was, until the invasion of fleetingly famous Aussie soap stars) that children would accept celebrities who might be beyond their field of experience – if they're good enough. Howerd enjoyed this immensely. 'Those kids didn't know I had been to Hollywood. Most of them didn't have a clue who I was, so it was a case of having to start from scratch and that's a healthy thing for any performer to do.'

There can be no resting on reputations in British panto, just three months of swirling chaos and altering scripts. Although an undoubted success, the show's sell-out status, which had initially stunned everyone involved, would be stunted by a series of hoax bomb alerts – London was reeling from a spate of IRA activity – and the arrival of the three-day week, which saw Britain lapsing into cold darkness during regular power cuts. Needless to say, lack of money and lack of electricity played havoc with the theatre industry, as it did elsewhere.

From darkness to light, though. Howerd was sent to Cyprus to 'lighten' the trauma for British troops locked in the conflict which followed the Turkish invasion. With hatred spinning around the island and with the British and United Nations Forces seemingly taking flak from every angle of this age-old conflict, Howerd found things difficult. He was relieved to be accompanied by the beautiful Julie Ege, recognized in an instant by most soldiers. (Even Greeks and Turks, it seemed. Some things are just universal.) Ege's disarming beauty seemed to soften the atmosphere, even in villages fraught with multitudinous and incomprehensible tensions. But it wasn't a pleasant trip. The British lads were clearly on a hiding to nothing and, with genuine fear in the air, a little light cabaret didn't seem particularly well placed.

Howerd's work rate was somewhat curtailed on his return. Ironically, just at the point when he felt reasonably relaxed, had money in the bank with no urgency for work and a legacy that would carry his fame for the rest of his life and, indeed, for much longer than that, he suddenly suffered from the nervous condition of spastic colon. It was hugely, painfully, instantly debilitating, causing him to double up in pain and, even more worrying, start to forget lines that had been previously cemented into his memory. This, of course, triggers a downward spiral, as the added anxiety of knowing that such attacks can occur at any time serves only to heighten them.

For Howerd, the mid-1970s were darkened by this curious condition – quite possibly the result of his years spent suppressing a natural state of nervousness, his professional tactic of pushing such fears into the background. Doctors informed him that such natural tensions can only be suppressed for so long, and they always return. This was the theory behind Howerd's mid decade retreat. The fact that he would conquer it is yet another tribute to the sheer drive that existed within him. How tempting must it have been to slink away to some rose-covered cottage in Dorset and live out the remainder of his life in rural tranquillity, entertaining the locals with dusty showbiz anecdotes, his ego floating on his legacy, his fame held aloft by endless repeats and his eternal appeal. How easy would that have been? But Howerd fought the illness courageously, and remained in view, and in work.

Up Pompeii wasn't dead. Perhaps it still isn't. Toward the end of 1999 a television screening of the first and best film created a minor stir as critics and public alike debated its worth. True enough, the whole affair seemed extraordinarily surreal, an echo from a world before the twin evils of political correctness and the post-PC laddish backlash had washed over us, heightening our cynicism. What seemed most extraordinary, however, was the rather quaint *Pompeii* paradox – the fact that, through such a mess of bawdy innuendo, and indeed many scantily clad diversions, shone such unexpected innocence. There were two further additions to *Pompeii*'s television history. In 1975, Talbot Rothwell was persuaded to emerge from retirement to script a 45-minute Easter Monday Special, produced by David Croft. And then, in Howerd's final year, 1991, came the curious *Further Up Pompeii*, a 'one off' recorded by London Weekend Television which ambitiously centred on a plotline that featured Lurcio, twenty years older than he had been at the end of the last series.

With Ray Milland in *The House in Nightmare Park*, 1973

In this particular plot, Lurcio was no longer a slave after being granted his freedom following his late master's will. But, in a plot twist that was staggering by *Pompeii*'s standards, it was revealed that Lurcio, as crafty as ever, had forged this aspect of the will and was open to blackmail from a devilish character. Not exactly Pinteresque but cleverly written by Paul Minett and Brian Leveson, who had been brave enough to grasp Rothwell's legacy and take it into uncharted territory. However, the show was far from satisfactory for a number of reasons. Firstly, obviously, it was completely out of step in a world that had discovered *Vic Reeves Big Night Out*. Not that there weren't a few similarities. And secondly, Frankie Howerd was now aged 74, plump and comparatively ungainly. Sad to say, his ageing stature did not help to enhance the slapstick nature of much of the comedy. Howerd's toga, once hilariously stupid, now looked merely sad. Also, at Howerd's insistence, it had been filmed

As the bishop in *Sgt Pepper's Lonely Hearts Club Band*, 1984

without an audience, thus depriving it of the spontaneity that had made it so special in the first place. Then there was the fact that Howerd, at his own admission, was drinking far too much for his own good. It transformed him into a complainer who shot fear through the younger cast members. It must be noted that his anger was mostly directed at himself for continuously forgetting his lines, although one mischievous parting gesture at the end of shooting was typically dark. After accepting a round of applause from the crew and production staff, Howerd responded by saying, 'Thank you. I have enjoyed working with all of you – except one.' And with that hanging marvellously in the air, he strode out of the studio leaving everyone guessing.

Frankie Howerd's weakest decade would undoubtedly be the 1980s. Scanning through his list of achievements it's painfully clear that his star faded during this tasteless though intriguing decade. There were a number of very good reasons for this. The Lurcio persona had, as I've said, been wiped by political correctness but it was difficult for Howerd to find a platform beyond this. He was also simply older than many people realized. Tiredness and the spectre of illness slowed his pace and he turned to the comforts of alcohol, though he was never an alcoholic, unlike so many of his peers. He was also unfortunate enough to feature in a number of projects that, through no fault of his own, flopped. Most notably his cameo in Robert Stigwood's almighty turkey, *Sgt Pepper's Lonely Hearts Club Band* flick. Presumably Howerd had been asked simply because of his previous appearances in Beatles films, not that this could be described as such. Even the non-pop literate mind of Howerd realized that the film was unforgivably sacrilegious, merely by taking the name of one of the greatest albums ever made, and he said as much on *Ask Aspel*.

Howerd was conspicuous by his absence from television. One would have thought some of the garishly-clad, spotty oiks dressed in New Romantic tartan and yellow leg warmers might have sensed the value in asking Lurcio, if not Howerd, to make a cameo appearance in their videos – but no. Then there was the non-appearance of the Second World War romp *Then Churchill Said to Me,* dropped from the schedules for fear of causing any offence so soon after

the war in the Falklands. When it was eventually screened, in the spring of 2000, it was greeted by unanimous apathy by critics and viewers alike.

As it turned out, *Then Churchill Said to Me* was merely disappointing and added up to little more than a second-rate stab at reincarnating the spirit of Lurcio in Private Percy Potts, a strongly Howerdian character drifting around Churchill's Internal Security Office. Clearly Potts was a good deal cleverer than his (largely stupid) superiors like Colonel Willesden and the absurd Sgt Major McKnuckles. The script was sub-*Pompeii* patter. 'Once I had St Vitus' dance and only the Gay Gordons turned up,' exclaimed Potts, setting the tone for this dispirited two-parter. As a vehicle for Howerd, it failed because the writers didn't allow him the space to develop the character, and he appeared to be pinned down by rigorous scripting: in *Pompeii,* Rothwell always made you feel as though Lurcio was taking the script any which way he chose, even if he wasn't. *Then Churchill Said to Me* was Howerd by numbers. As such it seemed cold, although in fairness the eighteen years that had lapsed since the actual production, during which British comedy had, for better or worse, exploded in just about every conceivable direction, hardly helped. That said, it could never emulate the huge and long-lasting success of the similarly-set *Dad's Army.*

Howerd's theatrical exploits fared rather better, however. He began the decade by proving that he was fully capable of adapting to more serious theatre by appearing with the English National Opera in *Die Fledermaus* at the Coliseum. He closed it with a hugely ambitious full national tour of his one-man show, *Frankie Howerd Bursts into Britain.* By this time it was interesting to see his name being rather noisily dropped by such modern-day stars as the emergent Vic Reeves and the more established Rik Mayall, Ben Elton and Rory Bremner, all of whom visited Howerd's stand-up show. He also managed to gain a sizeable cult following within Britain's ever lively university campuses. This was arguably due to his taking his show to them and the televising of the Oxford University date which appeared in 1990 as *Frankie Howerd on Campus,* filmed by London Weekend Television. In this extraordinary film, a sprightly and ferociously on-form Howerd was seen to tear through the precocious pomposity of Britain's finest. It was nothing short of triumphant and proved that Howerd could work effectively with an audience rather more accustomed to the comparatively sophisticated, though not necessarily funny, comic turns of the time. It would also be impossible to ignore the fact that Howerd's barren 1980s were effectively sliced in two by his 1986 return in *A Funny Thing Happened on the Way to the Forum,* which highlighted the prestigious Chichester Festival before moving to the Piccadilly Theatre. Compared to the show two decades earlier, it was a short-lived and rather too nostalgic affair. As such, it didn't set London alight – although Chichester was enriched and, to this date, the festival cites the show as one of its genuine coups, quite an achievement considering the power of the competition.

CHAPTER 14
THE 1990S

It is difficult to imagine how Frankie Howerd would have fared towards the end of the Millennium. When he died on 19 April 1992 at the age of 75 from a heart attack, he really had been appearing, despite his ill health, to be coming back into style. Perhaps it was the Oxford University show that eventually reversed the downward trajectory of his career during the 1980s. Perhaps it was just part of some natural comedic cycle and people were in need of a good daft old comedic romp. The stars gathered together, in person and in print, to heap inevitable praise on this most idiosyncratic comic talent. Roy Hudd called him 'flawed and fabulous, a ferocious talent trapped in a body that was merely human'. Neil Innes, who had co-starred in *Frankie Howerd Strikes Again* in 1981 called him 'beyond Python . . . a difficult bugger, too . . . ' If that seems a most unlikely tribute, consider that the British pop star Morrissey, a well-known aficionado of British comedy, once told the *Sounds* writer Dave McCullouch, 'I have the soul of Frankie Howerd.' (Whether that comment was laced with sarcasm or not is difficult to tell.) A more balanced view, perhaps, came from David Wigg, who wrote, in the *Daily Express;* 'Frankie's secret was that he could communicate with anyone and any age from Royalty to people with as humble an upbringing as himself.'

In the *Guardian*, Steve Dixon wrote, 'As a man he was a mass of complementary but usually conflicting neuroses.' Gary Bushell, writing in the *Sun*, said of him, 'One of the last original talents has left the planet.' Curiously, Howerd died within forty-eight hours of the death of that other very British television star, Benny Hill. Neither Hill nor Howard ever married, but while Hill died alone, Howerd was with friends and loved ones at the time of his demise. These included his sister Betty, who had always been there for her elder brother, offering support and advice but never attempting to share his spotlight, preferring instead to sit quietly in his shadow.

There was, of course, a star-studded memorial service for Frankie. Held late, on 8 July at St Martin-in-the-Fields, it attracted an impressive smattering of television talent, for once seemingly content not to jostle for the limelight that Howerd had so needed throughout his life. Barry Cryer, Howerd's great friend and a comedy writer and television personality in his own right, wrote and read a hugely evocative ode, which included these lines:

> Once more unto the speech, dear friends, once more,
> And sing in praise of Howerd, Francis,
> The tight-rope walker who always took chances,
> Always wobbling, never falling,
> Captivating and enthralling.
> Confiding, chiding but never crawling,
> Fearful, confident of his ability,
> Positively arrogant in his humility.

By the end Howerd had long since understood that his true genius lay in something very simple indeed: the ability to make people laugh. He had enjoyed his deeper moments, but it was the character of Lurcio that provided him with immortality. As ever though, Howerd would never allow anyone to think that making people laugh in the way he did was at all easy. His famously prickly character could surface at any time, and often did, making a mockery of people who were famous and even friendly to him, but who needed to know that he, Howerd, was in control. Witness his wonderful appearance on *Ask Aspel*, Michael Aspel's sweet chat show in 1991, when he gently chided the host with, 'Michael Aspel, the only man I know who can conduct an interview and sleep at the same time.' There was a lovely moment, preceding the interview, when the host had shown footage of Howerd entertaining the troops during that traumatic Borneo trip in the mid-1960s. In the clip, Howerd told the story of a butler called James who was summoned to his ladyship's bedroom. 'James . . . take off my shoes,' she ordered. 'Take off my stockings. Take off my dress . . . and don't ever let me catch you wearing them again.' Believe me, that joke was terrible even in the 1960s. But when Frankie Howerd told it on screen thirty years later, with his unique delivery, it was hilarious. And if he were around today, in this dubious new century of ours, he could tell it again and it would still make us laugh. In fact he could say nothing and have us in stitches. 'Ooooooh . . . No . . . listen, well . . . Ooooh, please yourself.' He was a truly unique talent and is sorely missed.

Frankie the rising star dining with a Hepburn look-alike for a press photo, early 1950s

FRANKIE HOWERD'S END BIT
BROADCAST AND THEATRICAL HISTORY

Radio highlights

Variety Bandbox,
 1946–1951

Fine Goings On,
 1951

Frankie Howerd Goes East,
 1951; BBC Radio Troop
 Entertainment Shows; Hong Kong,
 Borneo, Korea, Cyprus

The Frankie Howerd Show,
 1953

Television

The Howerd Crowd
 BBC (1st series); 1952; 3 x 60
 minutes
 Writer: Eric Sykes
 Producer: Bill Lyon-Shaw

Frankie Howerd's Korean Party
 BBC; 1952; 1 x 45 minutes
 Writer: Eric Sykes
 Producer: Kenneth Carter

Nuts in May
 BBC; 1953; 1 x 40 minutes
 With: Gilbert Harding, Carole Carr
 Writer: Eric Sykes
 Producer: Kenneth Carter

Tons of Money
 BBC; 1954; 1 x 40 minutes
 Writer: Eric Sykes
 Producer: Kenneth Carter

The Howerd Crowd
 BBC (2nd series); 1955; 2 x 60
 minutes
 Writer: Eric Sykes
 Producer: Ernest Maxin

Frankie Howerd
> BBC; 1956; 2 x 30 minutes
> Writers: Johnny Speight, Dick Barry
> Producer: George Inns

The Howerd Crowd
> ITV (ATV); 1957; 1 x 45 minutes
> Writer: Eric Sykes
> Producer: Brian Tesler

The Frankie Howerd Show
> ITV (ATV); 1958; 1 x 60 minutes
> With: Margaret Rutherford, Michael
> Denison, Sabrina
> Producer: Kenneth Carter

Frankie Howerd In ...
> BBC; 1958; 2 x 30 minutes
> Writers: Johnny Speight (episode 1);
> Reuben Ship/Phil Sharp (episode 2)
> Producer: Eric Miller

Frankly Howerd
> BBC; 1959; 6 x 30 minutes
> With: Sidney Vivian, Helen Jessop,
> Sam Kydd
> Writers: Reuben Ship/Phil Sharp
> Producer: Harry Carlisle

Ladies and Gentle-men
> BBC; 1960; 1 x 45 minutes
> With: Richard Wattis, Dennis Price
> Writers: Johnny Speight, Ray
> Galton/Alan Simpson, Barry Took
> Producer: Richard Afton

That Was The Week That Was
> BBC; 6 April 1963 (guest
> appearance)

A Last Word on the Election
> BBC; 1964; 1 x 25 minutes
> Writers: Frankie Howerd, Ray
> Galton/Alan Simpson, Frank
> Muir/Denis Norden, David Nathan,
> Dennis Potter
> Producer: Ned Sherrin

Frankie Howerd
> BBC; 1964–5; 6 x 25 minutes
> Writers: Ray Galton/Alan Simpson
> Producer: Duncan Wood

East of Howerd
> BBC; 1966; 1 x 50 minutes
> With: Shirley Abicair, Al Koran
> Producer: Joe McGrath

Frankie and Bruce
 ITV (ABC/Thames); 2 x 90 minutes
 (b/w); 1 x 60 minutes (colour)
 With: Bruce Forsyth
 Writers: Sid Green/Dick Hills
 (episodes 1–3), Barry Cryer
 (episode 3)
 Producers: Peter Dulay (episode 1),
 Peter Frazer-Jones (episode 2), David
 Bell (episode 3)

Howerd's Hour
 ITV (ATV); 1968; 1 x 60 minutes
 With: Hattie Jacques; Patrick
 Wymark
 Writer: Eric Sykes
 Producer: Keith Beckett

Frankie Howerd Meets the Bee Gees
 ITV (Thames); 1968; 1 x 65 minutes
 With: Arthur Mullard, Valentine
 Dyall, June Whitfield
 Writers: Ray Galton/Alan Simpson
 Producer: John Robins

The Frankie Howerd Show
 ITV (Thames); 1968; 1 x 50 minutes
 Writers: Sid Green/Dick Hills
 Producer: Peter Frazer-Jones

Frankie Howerd at the Poco à Poco
 ITV (Thames); 1969; 1 x 60 minutes
 With: Patrick Wymark
 Writers: Sid Green/Dick Hills
 Producer: William G. Stewart

The Frankie Howerd Show
 ITV (ATV); 1969; 6 x 45 minutes
 Writers: Sid Green/Dick Hills
 Producer: Sid Green

Up Pompeii
 BBC; 1969; 1 x 35 minutes (pilot)
 BBC; 1970; 7 x 35 minutes (1st
 series)
 BBC; 1970; 6 x 30 minutes (2nd
 series)
 With: Max Adrian (pilot & series 1),
 Wallas Eaton (series 2); Kerry
 Gardner, Walter Horsbrugh (pilot),
 Elizabeth Larner, Jeanne Mockford
 (series 1 & 2), Georgina Moon,
 William Rushton
 (series 1)
 Writers: Talbot Rothwell (pilot,
 series 1), Talbot Rothwell/Sid Colin
 (series 2)
 Producers: Michael Mills (pilot),
 David Croft (series 1), Sydney
 Lotterby (series 2)

Frankie Howerd: The Laughing Stock of Television
>   ITV (Thames); 1971; 1 x 60 minutes
>   With: Hattie Jacques, Peter Copley,
>   Patricia Hayes
>   Writers: Marty Feldman/Barry Took,
>   Ray Galton/Alan Simpson,
>   Talbot Rothwell
>   Producer: John Robins

Frankie Howerd's Hour
>   ITV (Thames); 1971; 2 x 60 minutes
>   Writers: Ray Galton/Alan Simpson
>   Producer: Peter Frazer-Jones

Whoops Baghdad
>   BBC; 1973; 6 x 30 minutes
>   With: Derek Francis, Jo Tewson
>   Writers: Sid Colin, David McKellar,
>   David Nobbs, Roy Tuvey, Maurice
>   Sellar, Peter Vincent, Bob Hedley
>   Producer: John Howard Davies

Frankie Howerd in Ulster
>   BBC; 1973; 1 x 45 minutes
>   With: June Whitfield, Wendy
>   Richard, Alan Cuthbertson
>   Writers: Ray Galton/Alan Simpson,
>   Chris Allen, Johnny Speight, Talbot
>   Rothwell, Roy Tuvey/Maurice Sellar
>   Producer: Terry Hughes

An Evening with Francis Howerd
>   BBC; 1973; 3 x 45 minutes
>   With: June Whitfield
>   Writers: Eric Merriman, Ray
>   Galton/Alan Simpson, Roy
>   Tuvey/Maurice Sellar, Tony Hare,
>   Peter Robinson, David McKellar,
>   David Nobbs, Mike Craig, Lawrie
>   Kinsley/Ron McDonnell,
>   Dave Freeman
>   Producer: John Ammonds

Howerd's History of England
>   BBC; 1974; 1 x 30 minutes
>   With: Patrick Newell, Patrick Holt,
>   John Cazabon
>   Writers: Barry Took/Michael Mills
>   Producer: Michael Mills

Francis Howerd in Concert
>   ITV (Yorkshire); 1974;
>   1 x 60 minutes
>   With: John Le Mesurier,
>   Kenny Lynch
>   Writers: Johnny Speight, Barry Cryer
>   Producer: Duncan Wood

Further Up Pompeii

BBC; 1975; 1 x 45 minutes

With: Mark Dignam, Kerry Gardner,
John Cater, Elizabeth Larner, Jeanne
Mockford, Leon Greene, Olwen
Griffiths, Jennifer Lonsdale, Cyril
Appleton, Lindsay Duncan

Writer: Talbot Rothwell

Producer: David Croft

Frankie Howerd's Tittertime

ITV (Thames); 1975; 1 x 60 minutes

With: Hughie Green

Writers: Barry Cryer, Ray
Galton/Alan Simpson

Producer: Peter Frazer-Jones

The Howerd Confessions

ITV (Thames); 1976; 6 x 30 minutes

With: Joan Sims

Writers: Hugh Stuckey/Peter
Robinson, Dave Freeman, Dick Hills

Producer: Michael Mills

This Is Your Life

ITV (Thames); 1976

Parkinson

BBC; 1978 (interview)

The Russell Harty Show

ITV (LWT); 1979 (interview)

Frankie Howerd Reveals All

ITV (Yorkshire); 1980;
1 x 60 minutes

With Henry McGee, Sheila Steafel,
Kenneth Connor

Writers: John Bartlett, Mike
Goddard, Laurie Rowley

Producer: Alan Tarrant

Frankie Howerd Strikes Again

ITV (Yorkshire); 1981;
6 x 30 minutes

With: Henry McGee, Neil Innes

Writers: John Bartlett, Mike
Goddard, Barry Cryer, Spike Mullins

Producer: Alan Tarrant

Then Churchill Said to Me

BBC; 6 x 30 minutes
(Originally scheduled for 1982:
cancelled and finally screened on UK
Gold, 1993)

With: Nicholas Courtney, Joanna
Dunham, Michael Attwell

Writers: Maurice Sellar/Lou Jones

Producer: Roger Race

Superfrank!
> C4; 1990; 1 x 60 minutes
> Writers: Vince Powell, Miles
> Tredinnick, Andrew Nickolds
> Producers: Cecil Korer/Derek Clark

Frankie Howerd on Campus
> ITV (LWT); 1990; 1 x 60 minutes
> Producer: Paul Lewis

Further Up Pompeii
> ITV (LWT); 1991; 1 x 45 minutes
> With: Joanna Dickens, Elizabeth
> Anson, John Bardon, Russell Gold,
> Peter Geeves, Roy Evans, Tim
> Killick, Gary Rice, Barry James
> Writers: Paul Minett/Brian Leveson
> Producer: Paul Lewis

Frankie's On . . .
> ITV (Central); 1992; 4 x 30 minutes
> Producer: Trevor McCallum

Films

The Runaway Bus (1953)
An Alligator Named Daisy (1955)
Jumping for Joy (1955)
The Ladykillers (1955)
A Touch of the Sun (1956)
Further Up the Creek (1958)
The Cool Mikado (1962)
The Fast Lady (1963)
East of Howerd (1965)
The Great St Trinian's Train Robbery (1965)
Carry On Doctor (1967)
Carry On Up the Jungle (1969)
Up Pompeii (1971)
Up the Chastity Belt (1971)
Up the Front (1972)
The House in Nightmare Park (1973)
Sgt Pepper's Lonely Hearts Club Band (1984)
HMS Pinafore (1985)
Trial by Jury (1985)

Theatre

Clacton (summer season, 1947)

Blackpool (summer season, 1949)

Out Of This World
(London Palladium, 1950)

Pardon My French (Prince of Wales
Theatre, London, 1953)

Charley's Aunt (Globe Theatre,
London, 1956)

Tons of Money (New Theatre,
Bromley, 1956)

A Midsummer Night's Dream
(Old Vic Theatre, London,
1958)

Mr Venus (Prince of Wales Theatre,
London, 1958)

Alice in Wonderland
(Winter Garden; Drury Lane,
London, 1960)

Puss In Boots (Coventry, 1962)

*A Funny Thing Happened on the
Way to the Forum* (Strand
Theatre, London, 1963)

Way Out In Piccadilly
(Prince of Wales Theatre,
London, 1967)

The Wind in the Sassafras Tree
(Coventry; Boston, USA;
Washington, USA; New York,
USA, 1968)

Jack and the Beanstalk (London
Palladium, 1973)

Cinderella (New Palace Theatre,
Plymouth, 1978)

Die Fledermaus (Coliseum,
London, 1981)

The Fly and the Fox (Churchill
Theatre, Bromley, 1984)

*A Funny Thing Happened on the
Way to the Forum* (Chichester
Festival and Piccadilly Theatre,
London, 1986)

Frankie Howerd Bursts Into Britain
(UK national tour, 1989)

Quite Frankly Frankie Howerd
(Lyric, Hammersmith and
Garrick Theatre, London, 1990)

PICTURE CREDITS

Photographs reproduced by permission of:

Hulton Getty (pages 28, 35, 67, 136)

Pictorial Press (pages 7, 11, 19, 22, 27, 31, 62, 71, 86, 94, 96-7, 98-9, 103, 111, 114-5, 126)

Mander & Mitchenson (16, 41, 59, 77, 85)

Ronald Grant Archive (15, 38, 42-3, 46, 51, 54, 64-5, 68, 78, 82, 90-1, 94, 109, 111, 118-9, 127, 129, 135)